Sparking Creativity in the World Language Classroom

Jam-packed with inspiring lessons and ideas, this book will help you access and enhance your own creativity in the classroom and inspire your students to become motivated language learners.

Top authors Blaz and Alsop share practical strategies to channel your creative impulses and transform them into effective lessons that will energize students of all levels. Aligned with ACTFL (American Council on the Teaching of Foreign Languages) and CEFR (Common European Framework of Reference for Languages) standards, the resources in this book support creativity as a practical process, with step-by-step guidance on goal-setting, implementation, evaluation, and feedback. Examples come from many world languages and cover fun and original topics, including tapping into students' own interests through cooking, memes, online videos, sports, arts and crafts, and more.

Relevant for all levels of language instruction, this text includes plentiful photocopiable charts, templates, and samples to use in the classroom.

Deborah Blaz has taught French to grades 7 through 12 for the past 44 years in Indiana, and has taught dual credit, AP, and college classes. She serves as world language department chair at her school and frequently presents workshops and keynotes, regionally, nationally, and internationally.

Tom Alsop's teaching career spans 58 years of service to the profession. After retiring from high school teaching, he taught Spanish at Butler University as an Adjunct for 23 years. Tom continues directing Spanish Teacher Summer Immersion Programs (*Aventuras Culturales*) in Madrid, Guadalajara, Mexico, and Havana, Cuba, and he hosts the Apple Podcast *Tom's World Language Cafe*.

Other Eye on Education Books Available from Routledge

(www.routledge.com/eyeoneducation)

The World Language Teacher's Guide to Active Learning
Strategies and Activities for Increasing Student Engagement, 3rd Edition
Deborah Blaz

Differentiated Instruction
A Guide for World Language Teachers, 2nd Edition
Deborah Blaz

The Antiracist World Language Classroom
Krishauna Hines-Gaither and Cécile Accilien

Your World Language Classroom
Strategies for In-Person and Digital Instruction
Rachelle Dené Poth

Enlivening Instruction with Drama and Improv
A Guide for Second Language and World Language Teachers
Melisa Cahnmann-Taylor and Kathleen R. McGovern

Leading Your Language Program
Strategies for Design and Supervision, Even If You Don't Speak the Language
Catherine Ritz

Differentiated Assessment for Middle and High School Classrooms
Deborah Blaz

The Ultimate Guide to Selling Your Original World Language Resources
How to Open, Fill, and Grow a Successful Online Curriculum Store
Erin E. H. Austin

Activities, Games, and Assessment Strategies for the World Language Classroom, 2nd Edition
Amy Buttner Zimmer

Sparking Creativity in the World Language Classroom

Strategies and Ideas to Build Your Students' Language Skills

Deborah Blaz and Tom Alsop

Routledge
Taylor & Francis Group
NEW YORK AND LONDON

Designed cover image: © Phive2015 Dreamstime.com

First published 2023
by Routledge
605 Third Avenue, New York, NY 10158

and by Routledge
4 Park Square, Milton Park, Abingdon, Oxon, OX14 4RN

Routledge is an imprint of the Taylor & Francis Group, an informa business

© 2023 Deborah Blaz and Tom Alsop

The right of Deborah Blaz and Tom Alsop to be identified as authors of this work has been asserted in accordance with sections 77 and 78 of the Copyright, Designs and Patents Act 1988.

All rights reserved. The purchase of this copyright material confers the right on the purchasing institution to photocopy pages which bear the copyright line at the bottom of the page. No other parts of this book may be reprinted or reproduced or utilised in any form or by any electronic, mechanical, or other means, now known or hereafter invented, including photocopying and recording, or in any information storage or retrieval system, without permission in writing from the publishers.

Trademark notice: Product or corporate names may be trademarks or registered trademarks, and are used only for identification and explanation without intent to infringe.

ISBN: 978-1-032-27549-9 (hbk)
ISBN: 978-1-032-25824-9 (pbk)
ISBN: 978-1-003-29325-5 (ebk)

DOI: 10.4324/9781003293255

Typeset in Palatino
by KnowledgeWorks Global Ltd.

Contents

Detailed Table of Contents...vii
Meet the Authors..xiv
Preface xvi

1. Why Be Creative?.. 1

2. The Creative Process from Start to Finish:
   Road Map to the Book 7

3. Curiosity: My Sparks 15

4. Imagination and Creativity 35

   Preliminary Chapter 5-Additional Information
   on Organization of Capsules: Goal Setting, Innovation,
   and *Implementation Capsules* 41

5. Modes of Instruction: Goal Setting, Innovation, and
   Implementation Capsules.. 43

6. Teaching Ideas: Goal Setting, Innovation,
   and Implementation Capsules.. 67

7. Promotional Ideas: Goal Setting, Innovation,
   and Implementation Capsules.. 95

8. Support: Making the Creative Journey Fun and Easy................ 117

9. The Path of Persistence: Creative Evaluation/
   How Did You Do?... 139

10. My Creativity Recipe Cards 151

11. Stimulating Creativity in My Students.. 223

12. Positivity, Celebration, and Final Thoughts 237

Appendix 271
Sources 273

NOTE: To locate specific activities quickly, please consult the Detailed Table of Contents following this section.

Detailed Table of Contents

Meet the Authors..xiv
Preface xvi

1. Why Be Creative?.. 1
   Introduction 1
   For Your Students 2
   For YOU 3
      You Are Unique 3
      Satisfaction 3
      Revitalization 4
      Life Skills 4
      Confronting Challenge 5

2. The Creative Process from Start to Finish: Road Map to the Book 7
   Introduction 7
   How to Read This Book 7
      First, a Little History 9
         The Six Steps to Success 9
         Mindsets Necessary Throughout the Process 10
      Necessary Mindset 11
         Positivity 11
         Goal-Setting and Manageability 12
         Risk-Taking 12
         Persistence 12
         Good Thinking Skills 13
         Support 13

3. Curiosity: My Sparks 15
   Introduction 15
   What Lights You Up? 15
   What Do I Like to Do? 16
      Arts 16
      Food/Cooking 18
      Games 18
         Games with a Ball 19
         Other Games 20

  Television Shows/Films 21
  Relaxation 22
 What Skills Do I Have? 22
  I Can Dance 22
  I Can Sing 23
  I Can Play Musical Instruments 23
  I Can Play a Sport 24
  I Can Play Video Games 25
  I Can Text 25
  Other Skills 26
 What Special Events Do I Look Forward To? 26
  Birthdays 26
  Parties With Friends 26
  Holidays and Vacations 27
 Stop and Think 28
 Use the Familiar: Personalization 30
  Personalize Using Your Life Events 30
   Why? 31
   Hot Seat 31
   Cognate Crush 32
  Personalize Using Students' Lives 32
   Never 33
  Personalize on a Broader Level 33

4. Imagination and Creativity 35
 Introduction 35
 Flights of Fancy 35
  Synectics 35
  Idioms 36
 Humor 37
  Internet as Inspiration 37
  Strategies from Stand-up Comedians 39
   Surprise 39
   Exaggeration 39
   Rule of Three 39
   Keep it Real 39

Preliminary Chapter 5-Additional Information on Organization of Capsules: Goal Setting, Innovation, and *Implementation Capsules* 41
 Introduction 41
 ACTFL Standards/Communication/Proficiency Levels 42

5. Modes of Instruction: Goal Setting, Innovation, and Implementation Capsules ... 43
Introduction ... 43
Capsule 1 – Lesson Planning ... 44
Capsule 2 – Seating Arrangements ... 46
Capsule 3 – Comprehensible Input (CI) ... 48
Capsule 4 – TPRS (Teaching Proficiency Through Reading and Storytelling) ... 50
Capsule 5 – Multiple Intelligences ... 52
Capsule 6 – Differentiated Instruction ... 54
Capsule 7 – Cooperative Learning ... 56
Capsule 8 – Peer Teaching ... 58
Capsule 9 – Team Teaching ... 60
Capsule 10 – Learning Stations ... 62
Capsule 11 – Pragmatic Approach ... 64

6. Teaching Ideas: Goal Setting, Innovation, and Implementation Capsules ... 67
Introduction ... 67
Capsule 1 – Vocabulary ... 68
Capsule 2 – Grammar ... 70
Capsule 3 – Culture/Holidays ... 72
Capsule 4 – Culture/Songs/Music ... 74
Capsule 5 – Culture/Foods ... 76
Capsule 6 – Culture/Famous Painters ... 78
Capsule 7 – Culture/Famous Writers ... 80
Capsule 8 – Culture/Sports ... 82
Capsule 9 – Culture/Dance ... 84
Capsule 10 – Games/APPS ... 86
Capsule 11 – Skits/Theater ... 88
Capsule 12 – Puppet Shows ... 90
Capsule 13 – Commercials ... 92

7. Promotional Ideas: Goal Setting, Innovation, and Implementation Capsules ... 95
Introduction ... 95
Capsule 1 – Talent Show ... 96
Capsule 2 – Podcast/Radio Show ... 98
Capsule 3 – Market Day ... 100
Capsule 4 – Dinner Theater ... 102
Capsule 5 – Language Carnival ... 104

Capsule 6 – Teacher/Student/Parent Travel 106
Capsule 7 – Prizes/Awards 108
Capsule 8 – Professional Development 110
Capsule 9 – Language Clubs 112
Capsule Name/Topic 114

8. Support: Making the Creative Journey Fun and Easy 117
Introduction 117
Human Sources of Support 1 – Teacher Colleagues 118
Human Sources of Support 2 – Students 119
Human Sources of Support 3 – Parents 120
Human Sources of Support 4 – Administrators 121
Human Sources of Support 5 – Community 123
Human Sources of Support 6 – Myself 125
Sources of Support 7 – Technology 127
    Using Technology to Spark Creativity 127
        Social Media for Ideas on Presentation
        and Collaboration 128
        Creating Content 131
Planning Page for Using Technology 137

**9. The Path of Persistence: Creative Evaluation/How Did
You Do?** 139
Introduction 139
Self-Assessment Card 1 – My Persistence 142
Self-Assessment Card 2 – Your New Creative
Teaching Strategies 143
Self-Assessment Card 3 – Your Support System 144
Self-Assessment Card 4 – Your Newest Super-Creative
Teaching Strategies 145
Self-Assessment Card 5 – Your Expectations 146
Self-Assessment Card 6 – Your Successes 147
Self-Assessment Card 7 – Your Failures 148
Self-Assessment Card 8 – Your Positivity 149
Self-Assessment Card 9 – Rewarding Others 150

10. My Creativity Recipe Cards 151
Introduction 151
Level 1 – Recipes 1–10 153
Alphabet – Creativity Recipe Card 1 153
Greetings-Farewells – Creativity Recipe Card 2 156

Weather Expressions – Creativity Recipe Card 3 159
Classroom Objects – Creativity Recipe Card 4 162
Food (to like) – Creativity Recipe Card 5 165
Clothing – Creativity Recipe Card 6 168
Present Tense Verbs – Creativity Recipe Card 7 171
Verb "to have" – Creativity Recipe Card 8 174
Christmas Carols – Creativity Recipe Card 9 177
TL Music – Creativity Recipe Card 10 180
Level 2 – Recipes 11–16 183
Shopping Spree – Creativity Recipe Card 11 183
Zoo – Creativity Recipe Card 12 186
Past Tense(s) – Creativity Recipe Card 13 189
Commands – Creativity Recipe Card 14 192
Dance – Creativity Recipe Card 15 195
Celebrities – Creativity Recipe Card 16 198
Advanced Levels – Recipes 17–22 201
Hospital – Creativity Recipe Card 17 201
Hotel Vocab – Creativity Recipe Card 18 204
Present Subjunctive – Creativity Recipe Card 19 207
Past Subjunctive – Creativity Recipe Card 20 210
Writer's Day – Creativity Recipe Card 21 213
Poetry – Creativity Recipe Card 22 216
My Own Recipes Created by ME 219

11. Stimulating Creativity in My Students 223
Introduction 223
Modeling 223
Strategies to Guarantee Creative Responses
from Students 224
RAFT 224
Placemats/Chat Mats 225
Choice Boards (Tic-Tac-Toe, sometimes called noughts
and crosses) 225
Creativity Starter 1 – Crazy clothes 227
Creativity Starter 2 – Serenade a student 227
Creativity Starter 3 – Silence, please 227
Creativity Starter 4 – Conga line 228
Creativity Starter 5 – Be a cheerleader 228
Creativity Starter 6 – Stand on the desk and recite poetry 228
Creativity Starter 7 – Classroom zoo 229
Creativity Starter 8 – Imaginary bus ride 229

Creativity Starter 9 – Ghost time 229
Creativity Starter 10 – Celebrity dress-up day 230
Creativity Starter 11 – Crazy commands.. 230
Creativity Starter 12 – Exercise 230
Creativity Starter 13 – Animal sounds.. 231
Creativity Starter 14 – Paper airplane... 231
Creativity Starter 15 – Spring cleaning... 231
Creativity Starter 16 – Zany incident.. 232
Creativity Starter 17 – Karate lesson... 232
Creativity Starter 18 – What's in the suitcase? 232
Creativity Starter 19 – Airplane pilot.. 233
Creativity Starter 20 – Art museum 233
Creativity Starter 21 – Beach day 233
Creativity Starter 22 – Dance time 234
Creativity Starter 23 – Great singer... 234
Creativity Starter 24 – Be a superhero 234
My Creativity Starter... 235

12. Positivity, Celebration, and Final Thoughts 237
Introduction... 237
Let's Get Started.. 237
Positivity – Celebration 1.. 239
   Teacher Colleague Support of the Year Award 239
Positivity – Celebration 2.. 239
   World Language Student Support of the Year Award 239
Positivity – Celebration 3.. 239
   World Language Parental Support of the Year Award 239
Positivity – Celebration 4.. 240
   World Language Administrative Support of the
   Year Award.. 240
Positivity – Celebration 5.. 240
   World Language Community Support of the
   Year Award.. 240
Positivity – Celebration 6.. 240
   World Language Creative Modes of Instruction of the
   Year Award.. 240
Positivity – Celebration 7.. 241
   World Language Creative Teaching Ideas of the Year Award 241
Positivity – Celebration 8.. 241
   World Language Promotional Ideas of the Year Award........... 241

Positivity – Celebration 9... 241
   World Language Teacher Creativity Starter of the
   Year Award... 241
Positivity – Celebration 10... 242
   World Language Teacher Creativity Improvement of the
   Year Award... 242
Positivity – Celebration 11... 242
   World Language Student Academic Achievement of the
   Year Award... 242
Positivity – Celebration 12... 242
   World Language Positive Attitude of the Year Award 242
Positivity – Celebration 13... 242
   World Language Creative Student of the Year Award 242
Positivity – Celebration 14... 243
   World Language Student Behavior of the Year Award 243
Positivity – Celebration 15... 243
   World Language Speaker of the Year Award 243
Positivity – Celebration 16... 243
   World Language Reader of the Year Award............................... 243
Positivity – Celebration 17... 244
   World Language Writer of the Year Award 244
Positivity – Celebration 18... 244
   World Language Grammar Student of the Year Award 244
Positivity – Celebration 19... 244
   World Language Student Techie of the Year Award 244
Positivity – Celebration 20... 244
   World Language Social Media Student of the Year Award...... 244
Positivity – Celebration 21... 245
   World Language Most Improved Academic Achievement
   of the Year Award.. 245
Positivity – Celebration 22... 245
   World Language Most Improved Student Behavior of
   the Year Award 245
Positivity – Celebration 23... 245
   World Language Culture Project of the Year Award................. 245
Final Thoughts 269

Appendix 271
Sources.. 273

Meet the Authors

Deborah Blaz, a French teacher at Angola High School in Angola, Indiana, received her B.A. in French and German from Illinois State University, a *diplôme* from the Université de Grenoble in Grenoble, France, and, in 1974, an M.A. in French from the University of Kentucky. Ms. Blaz has taught French and English to grades 7 through collegiate for the past 44 years in Indiana. She is department chair for World Languages at Angola High School in Angola, Indiana, and an adjunct for Ivy Tech University for dual credit classes.

Deb has published six books on language pedagogy as well as numerous articles in national and international language magazines, a chapter for a new book for beginning teachers, and was part of a translation team for an encyclopedia set. She is a keynote speaker and frequent workshop presenter.

Ms. Blaz was named to the All-USA Teacher team, Honorable Mention, by *USA Today* in 1998. She was also honored as the Indiana French Teacher of the Year in 1996 and received the Project E Excellence in Education award in 2000, the Dorothy S. Ludwig Excellence in Teaching, Secondary level award from the American Association of Teachers of French in 2020, as well as the Tom Alsop Distinguished World Language Publication/Research Award in 2020.

You can reach her at dblaz@msdsc.us.

Tom Alsop holds a B.A. in Spanish from Marian University in Indianapolis and an M.A. in Spanish Literature from Indiana University in Bloomington, Indiana. Tom also studied at the Pontificia Universidad Javeriana in Bogotá, Colombia.

Tom's teaching career spans 58 years of service to the profession. He taught middle school and high school Spanish for 35 years. The majority of that time, Tom taught at Ben Davis High School in Indianapolis. After retiring from high school teaching, he has taught Spanish at Butler University as an Adjunct for 23 years. Tom continues directing Spanish Teacher Summer Immersion Programs (*Aventuras Culturales*) in Madrid, Guadalajara, Mexico, and Havana, Cuba. Tom has an Apple Podcast, *Tom's World Language café,* and often presents at conferences around the country as well as doing workshops.

He is an accomplished author of more than 350 books/teaching materials that include Spanish readers, vocabulary, culture and grammar books, videos, and poster sets for Spanish teachers. Some of his books have been translated into French and German.

Tom was a past president of IFLTA, two-time president of the Indiana AATSP and served on the CSCTFL Board of Directors and the AATSP Sociedad Honoraria Hispánica (SHH) Advisory Board as regional director, vice-president and president.

During his career, Tom has been awarded a Rockefeller Fellowship, Lilly Teacher Creativity Fellowship, a Golden Apple Award, and the ACTFL Nelson Brooks Award for Excellence in the Teaching of Culture. Other awards that Tom has received during his career include the IFLTA World Language Teacher of the Year Award, the Indiana AATSP Teacher of the Year Award, the Ben Davis High School Teacher of the Year Award, and the Wayne Township Teacher of the Year Award. In 2017, Tom was inducted into the Salón de Enseñanza y Servicio by the Indiana AATSP. In 2020, the CSCTFL awarded Tom the Founders Award for his promotion of language learning, leadership, and dedication to the field of world languages. You can reach Tom at madridtomindy@gmail.com.

Preface

All the activities in this book are designed to be perfectly applicable to the American Council on the Teaching of Foreign Languages (ACTFL) World Readiness Standards for Learning Languages, as well as the Common European Framework of Reference for Languages: Learning, teaching, and assessment (CEFR) descriptors. Very basic overviews of both, in our own words, can be found below for your reference. Also, throughout the book, TL represents the target language being taught.

ACTFL Proficiency Levels Overview

Novice
Communicates in TL when prompted, and generally at single word or phrase level

Low	Mid	High
Uses single words or short lists of words.	Uses short phrases, no creative language.	Uses fragments and occasionally uses single sentences.

Intermediate
Communicates in TL autonomously, and at sentence level

Low	Mid	High
In predictable situations, always uses single sentences when required. Can create original phrases.	Always uses sentences, and occasional strings of sentences.	Uses strings of longer sentences with connector words and often uses descriptive words.

Advanced
Communicates in TL using well-formed narratives, using paragraphs and a variety of tenses

Low	Mid	High
Can use paragraphs and past and future tenses with minimal errors.	Can ask and answer questions and actively express opinions in all time frames.	With few errors, can deal with unexpected situations and express complex thoughts.

> **CEFR Proficiencies**
>
> The CEFR describes language proficiency at six levels: A1 and A2, B1 and B2, and C1 and C2. It also defines three "plus" levels (A2+, B1+, B2+)
>
> A1   Can talk about self and others, ask and answer questions using simple words and phrases
>
> A2   Can perform simple, routine tasks, using and understanding sentences in familiar situations
>
> A2+ Can understand the main points in a variety of formats (video, text, TV, spoken), follow instructions, tell a short story
>
> B1   Can describe experiences and events, opinions and plans using connected sentences and more than one tense, on a familiar topics or topics of personal interest
>
> B1+ Can ask and answer spontaneous questions, start a conversation and keep it going, complain, and give instructions in a fairly fluent manner. Can take notes while listening, express point of view using simple sentences, and understand most of what is heard.
>
> B2   Can interact with native speakers with some fluency and spontaneity. Can explain a viewpoint using evidence and elaboration.
>
> B2+ Can understand and respond to unfamiliar topics or opinions in detail, spontaneously ask an unprepared question, and read about unfamiliar topics, using a dictionary
>
> C1   In social, professional, and academic situations, can express ideas flexibly and effectively without much searching for words or phrases. Shows good use of connectors, patterns.
>
> C2   Very fluent and precise, can summarize information, and express self by using finer shades of meaning in complex situations

Levels A1 and A2 are also labeled as Basic User or Beginner, with A1 called Breakthrough and A2 as Way Stage. B1 and B2 are called Independent User or Intermediate, with B1 further described as Threshold and B2 as Vantage. Levels C1 and C2 are named Proficient User or Advanced, with C1 as Effective operational and C2 as Mastery.

Appendix A contains a chart showing correlations of these two as well as with the Common Core (CCSS) and Depth of Knowledge (DOK) standards.

Also, this book was co-written by two world language teachers, each with his/her own unique voice and experiences (Deb teaches

French at secondary level and Tom teaches Spanish at collegiate level). Each wrote the initial version of certain chapters, and then read the other's work, contributing ideas and critiques, but the initial author's vision still dominates most chapters. Here is a guide showing this aspect of the book:

Chapters 1, 2, 3 and 4 – Deb Blaz
Chapters 5, 6, 7, 9 and 10 – Tom Alsop
Chapter 8 parts 1–6 by Tom and part 7 (technology) by Deb
Chapter 11 – Strategies by Deb and Starters by Tom
Chapter 12 – Positivity celebrations by Tom and final thoughts by Deb
Deb also did this Preface and all the labeled standards for strategies and activities.

We hope you enjoy this book and that it proves very useful for you!

1

Why Be Creative?

Introduction

Contrary to popular belief, everyone has a creative streak. You are reading this book because you are already interested in enhancing (or discovering) your creativity, but perhaps you have not considered all the benefits you can derive from being creative. In this this chapter, you will learn how truly creative you can be!

Creativity has two different aspects in education because it applies to two groups at once: the teacher and the students. So, who benefits from creativity? This question has an easy and obvious answer: creativity benefits everyone, both teachers and students – but who benefits most? That is a tough question to answer as virtually no research has been conducted on this topic because creativity is hard to define and measure. However, we all know that the teacher is the driving force in any classroom, and because you obviously are motivated to become more creative, it should be obvious that the focus of this book is and should be on YOU! Just as in an airplane when oxygen masks drop down and you are instructed to put your mask on first and then help others, as a teacher, your focus should be on yourself first and then later on your students.

In this book, the next eleven chapters show how you can increase your creativity and reap the benefits both personally and professionally – for you, and for your students. Chapter 11 discusses strategies that help you stimulate the creativity in your students. Before we get down to the nitty-gritty on how to stimulate and use your creativity, let's look at the many benefits that increasing your creative ideas will bring to *you*.

There are great benefits to being creative in your personal life as well as elsewhere. As journalist and speaker Warren Berger says, "Creativity has this amazing power to give you renewed enthusiasm and energy – even in the most difficult circumstances."

For Your Students

You are probably thinking that you want to be (more) creative for your students. Creativity on your part has demonstrated benefits and can increase learning in your classroom. In addition to improving retention, using creativity boosts participation, promotes active learning, motivates students, and creates fun and positivity for you and your students. Your modeling of creativity as well as inspiring, teaching, instilling, and demanding it in your students will benefit them.

Being creative means a break from routine. Routine is a big component for successful classroom management, but too much of it will allow students to sit back and tune out. A bit of spontaneity now and then will require more attention and careful listening on the part of students. Students used to the same thing every day will not be able to rely on routine, and will be alert, waiting excitedly to hear what you will do or have them do next. Breaking routine can be a simple as changing the setting (class outdoors or an in-school walk). Any sort of movement enhances long-term storage and retention of material. You can also change what *you* do: stand in a different part of the room, or delegate some of your roles to your students.

Varying activities places more emphasis on students to notice, manipulate, and/or even plan how results will be displayed. This literally enhances brain cells and memory through mental stimulation and the social gratification of successfully completing something new or unusual. Again, this is easy to do: give students the choice between two things ("Which should we do first?") or ask for student feedback. Thank them for their help and you get another boost in their investment in your class.

Finally, if you harness and focus your creativity, it will show you how to do this for them. Chapter 11 gives some suggestions on how to implement creativity in class.

For YOU

But this book is about *you*, and that should be the focus, not something external (though being good at your job is personally rewarding, of course). The above, a desire for your students' gratification, is what any teacher should want but, since being creative is a bit of extra work (idea, planning, implementation), what's in it for you? Answer: happiness! Shawn Achor, author of *The Happiness Advantage*, states that when *you* do better, your students do better, not the other way around, and that happiness always precedes success. So, reason #1 for being creative is that it will make you happy.

You Are Unique

You have your own physical traits, personality, intellect, curiosity, imagination, goals, ideas, and expectations. Some of those you have in common with your friends, but the combination of all those details makes you distinctly different from others. Can we become creative if we recognize our uniqueness and take time to be different and celebrate that? Of course! Remember, variety is the spice of life. Light up your personality and share that light with others.

Satisfaction

Satisfaction is twofold: job satisfaction (as in having fun teaching and watching students learn) and personal fulfillment. Looking at the professional aspect first, bringing your personal enthusiasms and interests into your lessons will not only allow students to see you in a new light, but it will be easy (they're your interests, after all) and fun (you already enjoy them, so why not do more?) If you love a sport, have an artistic inclination, a musical talent, or just an obsession with a certain topic or person, use that! I love to learn the origins of people's last names, I make things using origami, I can play the nose flute, and I know how to read palms…all things I incorporate in lessons at one time or another.

Now for the personal benefits: the next time you are in a museum staring at a masterpiece on the wall, don't just say "I wish I could do that." Try to simply appreciate what it took to generate such brilliant work and ask yourself what it is that *you* can create. Research shows that just being in the presence of artistic genius can be good for your health. But it is even better if you can do it, too. A common misconception is that creativity is artistic (books, music, etc.) – but anything can be looked at with a creative mind. Creativity can be deployed anywhere and on anything: a spreadsheet can become a plaything, a PowerPoint can be looked at as a canvas, and so on. The same advice is good also for comparing yourself to other teachers: don't say "I wish I were as creative as X," but instead, find, explore, and enjoy your own creativity.

Creativity is personally fulfilling and useful, and seeking stimulation for creativity can also be enjoyable. Things like reading, writing, knitting, baking, listening to music, and other enjoyable activities can open your imagination and result in something wonderful. How to seek your creativity "sparks" is discussed in more detail in Chapter 3.

Revitalization

Brain research shows creativity can lift your mood, lower stress, boost your immune system, and lower your blood pressure, possibly prolonging your life (see "Creativity Predicts a Longer Life" https://www.scientificamerican.com/article/open-mind-longer-life/). Doing any activity you enjoy might actually make you healthier (and it definitely will make you happier).

Routine can also get boring for you. Delegating some of your duties (such as choosing an assistant to make decisions for you and the class, write on the board, explain a topic, look up vocabulary, and so on) will free you from boring everyday duties as well.

I think we all have and look forward to doing special lessons or units with our students – something different, a change of pace. And who would not like to have students paying better attention to you, as novelty increases their interest?

Compliments and smiles are common results when you do something creative. Positive feedback from students for your creative efforts gives us a pat on the back for work well done as well as shows us what they enjoy so we can do that more often. Just ask questions that encourage positive responses: What did you enjoy most? What is a new word you learned? etc.

Life Skills

Creativity also involves skills that are necessary to be successful – in life and in a career.

- It builds problem-solving skills (finding a new way to do a task, for example).
- Being able to see the big picture and not get lost in the details is important in many areas of life. Being creative and letting your mind wander wherever it goes instead of focusing on just one thing can lead in amazing directions.

- It also makes us more open-minded and patient with others. Learning to accept new or different ideas and look at ordinary things more deeply makes us better thinkers and prepares us to take on challenges.
- Creativity is a method for handling pressure. It works on two different levels. One is purely the fact that it can help you succeed; the other is that it energizes you, making you feel like you want to push forward, even when times are tough.

Confronting Challenge

Trying something new can be a bit scary, but if you succeed, it can be wonderful. I always like to remind people of these sayings:

- Henry Ford said, "If you *always* do what you've *always* done, you'll *always* get what you've *always* got."
- Author and journalist Gail Sheehy said, "If we don't change, we don't grow."
  And my own personal motto:
- While change does not always bring improvement, there is NO improvement without change.

If being creative helps you see the big picture, stay motivated, and solve problems, nothing could boost your confidence more. When you think creatively and overcome challenges, you realize how capable you really are.

Very few good things in life come without some effort. Studies show that creative people see challenges as something they can overcome, rather than stressful things they cannot get past.

Fill in the blanks after reading this chapter:

What I most want to gain from being creative: _____

What in this chapter did I find most motivating? _____

Refer back to your answers above any time you find your energy flagging a bit. Don't forget to ask for help from others when needed, too. Sometimes it "takes a village" to get there!

2

The Creative Process from Start to Finish
Road Map to the Book

Introduction

Should you read the chapters in this book in order, from cover to cover? *Not at all!* Skip around to delve into the part or parts that you feel you need. It is not expected that you read the whole book… at least, not all at once! Each chapter focuses on a different aspect of creativity, and it is likely that you will go straight to the part that you want and need most. When you have mastered that aspect of your creative life – and you WILL! – then begin to look at other chapters. Each chapter can be read as a stand-alone on its topic, and each chapter has, at the end, space for you to record the creativity ideas generated while reading, as well your reflections.

How to Read This Book

Here is a quick guide to what is in each chapter, to help you decide where you should start:

Chapter 1 deals with the personal benefits you will experience as you enhance the creative aspects of your life: renewed energy, happiness, and health, among others.

Chapter 2 introduces both the book and a general view of the basic concepts involved in being more creative. This chapter is a good introduction to the mindset needed to be more creative (such as a willingness to take risks in trying new things and how to persist if not instantly successful) and the other elements to put into place, for example: a good support system, how to ask for help, how to start with a goal, and how to measure success. This could be a good starting point for a group doing a book study together, or a department chair using this book to lead professional development.

Chapter 3 begins with a personal inventory of skills and enjoyable activities and focuses on how to use real-life activities that you enjoy or personal life events and perspectives in a creative manner. There are many examples of how to use art, music, and other creative things you already enjoy doing, and share them with others. Other topics included are using celebrations and daily life as well as unusual events and current events to be creative.

Chapter 4 deals with using strategies to stimulate your imagination to reach outside your current boundaries, such as humor strategies from standup comics, idioms in the target language, and an industry creativity-enhancing method called synectics.

Chapter 5 begins instruction on goal setting, a key to success. This chapter deals with modes of instruction such as seating, learning stations, differentiated instruction, and more. This chapter includes 11 capsules that serve as an action plan to implement and teach new world language learning ideas and concepts as well as a template.

Chapter 6 continues the capsules concept with 13 capsules on teaching ideas incorporating creative ways to teach grammar, vocabulary, and culture. A template is included.

Chapter 7 completes the capsules by discussing nine ideas for promoting the study of world languages, world language clubs, and professional development. A template is included.

Chapter 8 reviews seven sources of support to rely upon in implementing your ideas (students, parents, administration, people from your community, technology, etc.), with an action plan for each. Templates to guide you in using this support make it fun and easy.

Chapter 9 highlights the importance of persistence; not every first effort is a total success. Nine self-evaluation reflection guides are included: what worked, what could be better, and how to make each idea a success.

Chapter 10 contains 22 recipe cards for creative ways to teach verbs, vocabulary, and culture to levels 1, 2, and advanced.

Chapter 11 changes the focus to stimulating student creativity, with a variety of methods followed by 24 creativity starter ideas you can use almost immediately to make your students think in more creative ways.

Chapter 12 discusses how to commemorate the good things that come with using more creativity. There are 23 different award certificates to use as well as ideas for the celebrations at which to present the certificates. Last are some final thoughts and advice about creativity to end the chapter.

The **detailed Table of Contents** will also be a good resource to quickly and easily locate any idea you remember reading about.

First, a Little History

Creativity in teaching has become a subject of interest to researchers in the last couple of decades. It is generally considered highly desirable, if not necessary. As a trait, it is associated with advantages in life, both personally and professionally.

Despite its perceived importance, there have been few studies on how creative teachers think, work, and function in the classroom. One of the problems is that there is not one consistent definition of what creativity is and how it relates to effective teaching.

There are many studies on the strategies used in a creative classroom, but those focus only on the specific strategy. We will reference many, if not all, of those in this book, but the process itself must be discussed first to establish a definition of creativity as we the authors view it, and how to achieve it.

The Six Steps to Success

1.	Curiosity	Chapter 3
2.	Imagination	Chapters 3 and 4
3.	Creativity	Chapters 3 and 4
4.	Goal setting	Chapters 5, 6, and 7
5.	Implementation	Chapters 6, 10, and 11
6.	Evaluation and feedback	Chapters 8 and 9

Mindsets Necessary Throughout the Process

- Risk-taking
- Support
- Persistence
- Positivity

Curiosity: All great thinkers from the beginning of time have been curious. Curious people deviate from textbook prescriptions and traditions and ask questions. From Plato, Shakespeare, and Columbus to Dr. Martin Luther King Jr., Marie Curie, Steve Jobs and more, the common thread to their success is curiosity. Observations of the world around them generate curiosity, and then creativity follows.

Imagination: Everyone is born with an imagination. Imagination is vital in social-emotional development. Albert Einstein said, "Imagination is more important than knowledge." Imagination allows us to think of things that aren't real or around us at any given time. Imagination also involves emotion: first, being in the right mood to imagine, and then the feelings such as wonder, pleasure, and fun, generated by those things imagined. Imagination is a kind of flexibility and energy in thought.

Creativity: Imagination is sometimes confused with creativity, but they are actually different. Imagination is the door to possibilities; creativity involves problem-solving. To be creative, you have to do something. It's a very practical process. Imagination generates the thought and creativity decides what form and action(s) will be used. If there are no action items to follow, it will be just a dream that flies away in the wind.

Goal setting: In using creativity, people plan – intentionally or unintentionally. Goal setting should include listing necessary steps and supplies needed, setting a reasonable timeline (as detailed as possible), breaking down steps into tiny positive steps forward, as well as planning for evaluation both during and after achieving the goal. Creative goals will not happen if they are not specific…but the goals should focus on process rather than concrete goals. For example, in writing this book, my goal was to write a certain number of pages each day instead of "write a chapter," which would seem too overwhelming.

Implementation: Patience and persistence are essential in implementation: don't rush through or skip steps; each are important. Be willing to adjust the initial time goal if setbacks are encountered. Also, in implementation, a creative activity should have the following:

- A real need (is it worth doing?)
- Buy-in and collaboration (involve others' needs and interests, and their support)
- A tangible result (what will we see/get?)

Implementation involves a pitch, steps to be taken, knowing who will take them, knowing who will be held responsible, and an end result. It should also involve plans for revision and refinement as needed.

Evaluation: Evaluation can be done during the process (formative) or after it is complete (summative). It may be done via self-assessment, peer review, or group assessment. It is a time of reflection where you look back at the original idea and see if the current form or result is in line with the original vision. Have in mind what success in this endeavor should look like, and how to measure that so you know when to celebrate!

Necessary Mindset

There are several things needed for success in creativity. The first is the right mindset. It may seem funny to see this in a book focused on showing the skillsets necessary to be creative, but your mindset is the easiest to change, and will have a huge impact on your creativity.

High-achieving people have several mental habits that differ from the 92% of people who do not achieve their creative goals. The successful 8% have several mindsets in common:

Positivity

First, and *most important*: identify any negative thoughts, and push the pause button on those. Don't hesitate or second-guess your first creative impulse. Second, force yourself to have positive thoughts: "I can do this." Or "I am a creative person." Shawn Achor in *The Happiness Advantage* writes, "…our brains are literally hardwired to perform at their best, not when they are negative or even neutral, but when they are positive." Positive thoughts enhance our consideration of new possibilities, which is essential to the creative process.

An important part of positivity is the aspect of celebration. Every time you take one step forward in the process, reward yourself. Buy a fancy coffee or tea, make your favorite dessert, watch a movie/play/concert, go for a walk (or any other outdoor activity you enjoy), go on a dollar store shopping spree, take a soothing bath, watch silly videos on social media, listen to music, dance, do a sport, ride a bike – you know what you like; do it!

Goal-Setting and Manageability

Many people become inspired by something someone else did and want that result as well. The first step should be to ask yourself: What do I want to accomplish? How will this benefit me/my students? And then: how will I know when I have achieved my goal?

One of the mistakes many people make is to not break down the goal into small, easily achievable *positive* steps. Doing this and focusing on just one step at a time will make the process much easier and less overwhelming. Setting small, attainable goals for yourself will first build a good skill base and create momentum, where things then get easier and more natural. And don't forget to build in small rewards for yourself each time you accomplish a step toward your goal.

Risk-Taking

Pablo Picasso said, "I am always doing that which I cannot do, in order that I may learn how to do it." Researchers found that an international sample of people who were willing to take intellectual risks (meaning trying new things with the possibility they might fail) were more likely to believe that they could be creative, were more likely to engage in creative activities, and had more creative achievements than people who did not take risks.

Eleanor Roosevelt challenged people to do something that scares them, every day. Perhaps that is excessive. Risk-taking does not need to be constant or frequent, just occasional, but the willingness must be there to be truly creative.

Looking back to the 8% of people who achieve their goals: they prepare mentally to fail. They admit it will happen. Give yourself permission to fail; it will take a lot of the pressure off, and now you will be ready to learn, adjust, and keep moving forward.

Would you be more willing to rack up mistakes if you knew you had to make a certain number of them to get to a prize? This is you when being creative.

Persistence

Persistence is the biggest difference between creative people and those who are not. It is the most important aspect in achieving creativity: Try and fail; learn and grow…you will get there! Successful creative teachers seek feedback and make adjustments during the learning activity. This quality and how to encourage it in yourself if described in Chapter 6.

Good Thinking Skills

Creative people need to think on three different levels: synthetic, analytic, and practical. Synthetic thinking (Chapters 3 and 4) involves generating new and interesting ideas, for example, making connections between things that others have not seen. The other two levels are part of the evaluation process. Analytic thinking will distinguish good ideas from those not worth pursuing. Thinking analytically would involve working out the implications of an idea and testing it. Practical thinking skills are used to convince others that an idea is worthy and that it has a potential audience and use. All three are needed for success.

Support

Creativity is not necessarily done in a vacuum. There is no shame in seeking support groups of people working on a similar topic or skill or asking for feedback on an idea, lesson, or unit. Support groups and feedback will be discussed more in Chapter 6.

The chapter I want to check out FIRST: _____
Why I chose that chapter to begin with: _____
_____
What step I think I am already good at: _____
What step do I think I will have the most success in using? _____
What mindset should I focus on first? _____

3

Curiosity
My Sparks

Introduction

This book is about you: you are ALREADY so creative, but perhaps don't realize it. Here you will learn to list and harness your creative impulses in SO many ways! Use your skills (physical and mental) as well as activities – everyday ones or unusual ones – in more creative ways than ever and share them with others in new ways. Each section begins with a reflection piece followed by ways to flesh out and apply things you enjoy and are good at. This adds creativity and variety for your students and enjoyment for all!

What Lights You Up?

One of my favorite motivational sayings:

> AN UNLIT CANDLE CANNOT LIGHT ANOTHER

So, what lights <u>you</u> up? Ask yourself:

- What do I really like to do?
- What am I good at?
- What do I look forward to doing?

I really like to do this:	1.
	2.
I am good at this skill:	1.
	2.
I look forward to doing this <u>special</u> thing:	1.
	2.

Then, when you have the answers on this grid, ask yourself: how can I use this in class?

What Do I Like to Do?

Shawn Achor in his book *The Happiness Advantage* talks about what he calls the "Tetris Effect," which tells us to learn to spot patterns of possibilities so we can seize those when we see them. That is what this chapter is all about. You have just listed some of your possibilities that you could act on. Next is to find happiness and that happiness will, in turn, lead to success. Let me share with you what I would list in that grid, and what those skills have led me to do as a teacher. In this chapter "I" and "me" refers to only one author; we wanted to show you ways of using the above grid successfully.

Arts

Using myself (Deb) as an example: I like to make things (crafts), so I search for opportunities to do things like that. For National French week, we make red, white, and blue bead creations to wear to represent the language we are taking that then initiate discussions with other students about the class and subject matter. We also decorate all the lockers in the school with positive comments in the target language (TL), with the same results: students ask others for help in reading them, and our notes stay up for months as they are much appreciated.

> **ACTFL:** Culture, all proficiency levels, even when done in TL; **CEFR:** A2

When studying Paris, we might use a template to carve a bar of Ivory soap into a replica of the Arc de Triomphe while studying Napoléon's victories and legacy, or appreciate the challenges Eiffel faced in constructing his tower by building our own out of spaghetti and mini marshmallows.

We can make floats for Mardi Gras that illustrate aspects of Cajun or Francophone culture or decorate tissue boxes with cultural topics (which are then on display throughout the year as we use the contents).

Spanish classes make papel picado, cascarones, piñatas, ofrendas, alebrijes, or paper flowers using crepe paper. This year as we studied the monarch butterfly migration, we learned a song and made small butterfly puppets to use as we taught elementary school classes.

Here is a list of arts and crafts for the classroom which you could consider using (Figure 3.1):

Figure 3.1 Crafts for the classroom

album	mask
alebrijes (Mexican folk art)	mobile
apparatus	model
award	mosaic
banner	mural
board game	necklace or other jewelry
booklet	needlework
bookmark	ojos de dios
calendar	origami
card game	painting
cascarones	papel picado
castanets	paper flowers
ceramic	papier-maché
clothing/costume	piñata
collage	poster
design a structure	printing or stamping
new product	punched tin art (Mexico)
new animal	puppet show
diorama	quilt
finger puppet(s)	rainstick
flag	sashiko (Japanese decorative stitching)
flipbook	scrapbook
furniture	scroll
gadget	sculpture
greeting card	sign
hand puppet	silk screen
hat	stencil
invitation	stick puppet
jigsaw puzzle	tee-shirt (painted or dyed)
kite	toy
knitting	wall hanging
macramé	weaving
marionette	woodcut

Food/Cooking

What else do I like to do? Cook (and eat).

As you read a story in class, if food or drink is involved in the story, try to offer that experience to others. While the first-year classes were reading a book about a girl who goes to Paris, we made crepes with Isabella as she does in her adventures in Paris. Food is a great opportunity for cross curricular teaching: the FACS (family and consumer science) classes make our crepe batter for us, and I teach them, along with my students, how to flip a crepe into the air and catch it – a good example of a lesson/skill they can use for the rest of their lives. Am I nervous as I demonstrate this skill? You bet. If I mess it up, do I die of embarrassment? This is a good chance to model how to accept failure and put it into perspective: "There is always more batter," "Be careful to keep the pan horizontal. See what happened when I didn't?" and so on. Don't try to be perfect; just model having fun.

> **ACTFL:** Culture, all proficiency levels; **CEFR:** A2 for task; if questions after, ACTFL: Communication, Novice Mid; CEFR: A1. If doing associated readings or videos, ACTFL: Novice High; CEFR A2+ and B1

We also did a cheese tasting with Isabella (she hated Roquefort, and most of my students did, too). During a unit about Quebec, we try *sucre en creme* or *poutine*, both traditional dishes. And we celebrate the new spring holiday, Gout de France, according to whose traditional practices students choose recipes, cook the dishes, and enjoy them all together as a tasting menu in courses.

Spanish classes learn about the history of chocolate and may sample that and/or how to use a *molinilla* to make hot chocolate. Our classes learned about *horchata* and how to make it. Have a guest come in and show how to make tamales, churros, or another dish they'll love.

Kids love to taste new things. Make it a game: buy several different flavors of chocolate, give each a small piece and have them guess the flavor. Buy some TL sweets and have them rate their favorites (by the way, there are some cute videos on YouTube of Americans tasting unfamiliar foreign foods or of TL people tasting American foods).

Games

I also really like to play games: card games, board games, throwing games (like *pétanque*).

What types of games did you play when younger? Group games, one-on-one, or individual ones? What do you (or your own children, if applicable) like to play now? Maybe even better: what types of games do TL children like to do? See if you can incorporate those into a lesson. Not video games, but physical ones. Movement encourages long-term retention, and enjoyment while doing the activity boosts retention even more.

Games with a Ball

Connections: Announce a topic that could have many different responses, such as colors, sports, things you like or do not like, etc. For an example, choose things you like or do not like, hold a ball of yarn, and start the topic with an appropriate word. Ask who would like the word I mentioned, and toss them the yarn. When they catch it, they must repeat your word, add theirs, and then throw it to someone else who declares they also like that thing (and will add a new thing as well). This continues, unwinding the yarn and throwing it until everyone has had it, repeating all the vocabulary from everyone along the way. When everyone has had a turn, wind the ball back up, retracing the words each has chosen. This is a great teambuilding activity, and you get to know your students better as they also see their connections to each other.

ACTFL: Interpersonal, Novice Low; **CEFR:** A1

In this same game, if "colors" are chosen as a topic, use a blow-up beach ball or any multicolored ball. The student catching the ball must say the color their thumb touches when they catch it.

Grand Prize Game: this comes from my favorite childhood TV show, *Bozo the Clown*. Students must answer a question to get a chance to toss a ball into a series of buckets, each of which is a bit farther away from the next, to earn points for their team.

ACTFL: Interpersonal, Novice Mid; **CEFR:** A1

Spelling Ball: name a word, phrase, or sentence and each student catching the ball says the next letter (students who misspell are "out").

ACTFL: Interpersonal, Novice Mid; **CEFR:** A1, A2

Description Dodgeball: Use a soft ball as students will be trying to hit each other! Call out a description (tallest, short hair, blue shorts, smart, etc.) and the student with the ball tries to hit a student fitting that description by throwing the ball. If they hit the student, that person now gets the ball. Note: students could also wear name tags as different animals, cities, etc. to be described instead of personal traits.

> **ACTFL:** Interpretive, Novice High;
> **CEFR:** A2

Basketball dare: This works on practice commands. A student tries to put a ball through a hoop. If successful, they can tell YOU (or a classmate) to do something. (Be sure to lay out the ground rules ahead of time, such as no shouting or leaving the room, nothing too embarrassing, etc.)

> **ACTFL:** Communication, Novice High;
> **CEFR:** A2

Other Games

I just read a blog by a language teacher who does a variety of activities using a colored parachute. One example is to have everyone holding the edges lift the chute high and pull it downward to make a mushroom shape. One student calls out information in the TL such as "plays tennis" and everyone who fits that description must run inside the parachute while the others continue to lower it.

> **ACTFL:** Interpretive, Novice High; **CEFR:** A2 unless specified otherwise

I bought very inexpensive wood miniature Jenga sets and numbered the blocks. My students must answer a question or perform a task in the TL before moving a block. Make a list of Jenga activities for every unit, and store the sets in quart-sized plastic bags for spontaneous use or as part of a learning center activity.

Don't forget jumping games like jump rope, hopscotch, or check the TL culture for others (find TL chants used for jumping games). Chasing/running games are also fun: many cultures have variations on Duck Duck Goose, Red Light Green Light, or Hide and Seek that could be adapted for your classroom. Hand games (check for TL authentic ones) like cat's cradle or clapping games are also well received by students.

> **ACTFL:** Culture, Novice Mid; **CEFR:** A2

Figure 3.2 Well known games to adapt for the classroom

Bingo	I'm Thinking of a Number
Charades	Jeopardy
Fly Swatter	Musical Chairs
Four Corners	Pictionary
Hangman	Scattergories
Heads Up, 7Up	Scavenger Hunt
Hot or Cold	Taboo (or Password)
Hot Potato	Would You Rather?

Figure 3.2 has a list of beloved childhood games to consider using (and putting your own spin on by incorporating your own vocabulary, classroom jokes, student and teacher names, etc.).

Television Shows/Films

Let your favorite shows (or the students' favorites) enter your classroom. Game shows are the easiest, with you as the host, and students arranged into teams. Think of classic games like Password, Wheel of Fortune, or Jeopardy. I have also done versions of The Dating Game using the inside-outside circle format to talk about foods, sports, and other topics. One

> **ACTFL:** Communication, Novice High; **CEFR:** A2+

year, I themed the whole year as a version of Survivor, with students performing a series of tasks I designed (whenever I could think of one). Family Feud can be done after a survey activity ("My parent think I do this too much" "I wish I knew how to…" etc.) Who Wants to Be a Millionaire is good for review (complete with phone-a-friend and other tactics). Why not do a classroom version of the Masked Singer (but maybe the Masked Speaker) or any other that inspires your creative urge!

The same is true for movies. Take movies you (or they) enjoy and use them. Enthuse about your favorite actors, TL or not (the kids will love to tease you about this but make them do it in the TL). When minions first appeared, I used them whenever possible, in stories, worksheets, and other activities. We have had debates on which Marvel hero is the best, or Marvel versus DC comics, and I had my level 1 students, as a summative for first semester, recreate themselves as a superhero and tell me about themselves: looks, favorites, family etc. Ratatouille and The Little Prince have also contributed many ideas to use in my classroom. When a new movie is about to come out starring my favorite actors or set in a TL country, this is a great chance to show them a trailer for it in the TL or to tell them the basic plot as a story (written or oral). This is a high-interest activity, guaranteed.

Relaxation

I also really enjoy just doing nothing. Teachers all need some down time and, it turns out, this is absolutely the BEST way to have your most creative moments. Letting my mind go somewhat blank, daydreaming, and with fewer distractions, ideas come in and sometimes make connections I would not have thought of. A 2009 study by the Department of Psychology at the University of British Columbia found that daydreaming is a good way to boost creativity. Think of Isaac Newton sitting beneath his apple tree when the idea of gravity literally fell on him. There are many stories of people who had a great idea just as they were about to fall asleep.

You don't have to be completely immobile or practicing mindfulness for this to happen though; just zoning out while doing something routine but boring (washing dishes, folding laundry) or, even better, out in nature and away from screens and phones are great creativity boosters. I often think of the Swiss engineer Georges de Mestral walking his dog and afterward detangling burrs from its coat, which gave him the idea for Velcro as he observed how the burrs adhered to the dog's hair.

Yoga and mindfulness are very beneficial to education. When I began doing mindfulness with my students, their quiz scores jumped by 29%. There is a lot of evidence for other good benefits, and it isn't hard to find exercises to meditate or relax in your TL.

> **ACTFL:** Interpretive, Novice Mid; **CEFR:** A2

What Skills Do I Have?

Creativity is much simpler if it is something you are already good at or enjoy. Ask yourself what skills you can share. I know how to read palms, which comes in handy when we learn the future tense. Note: I do not have all these skills; this section just anticipates some you may have listed.

I Can Dance

I have a past as a belly dancer and that is not something I am willing to personally demonstrate to students. However, I can bring in my zills (finger cymbals) when we study Francophone countries of North Africa and show them a how-to video in case they'd like to try.

> **ACTFL:** Culture, Novice Low; **CEFR:** A2+

If you are listening to music in connection with a lesson (and there are LOTS of lists of songs that correlate with grammar out there), search on YouTube for the song name, a plus sign, and the word for choreography in the TL. I often find some kids or professionals who have choreographed a song we are studying, and we can pair music and movement for a great brain break. If you can find someone, invite a dance instructor or talented parent or other local in to give a lesson to students: the merengue, the macarena (Spanish), ballet steps or square dancing (French), a waltz or maypole dance (German) are just a few culturally authentic things to teach. If you can join in, in my experience, students really appreciate that as well and feel less like they are being studied or graded in some way.

I Can Sing

Life is cooler if you sing more (and so is your class). When singing, you tend to lose any strong foreign accent, so if you can sing, sing as often as you can! Sing children's songs (alphabet, counting and more), grammar songs (I made my own up using popular tunes), and holiday songs (we go caroling to the middle school and a nearby grade school – a great opportunity for my students to see favorite teachers from their past, show off their linguistic skills, and recruit future students). Music is portable (my students teach it to their families, download it to listen to on their own time, etc.) and it doesn't just improve pronunciation. Music helps retain vocabulary (and it is vocabulary in context) and structures in the brain. And it is a lot more fun than drills or worksheets.

ACTFL: Culture, all levels; **CEFR:** A2

If you can't sing, can you rap? Anything done with rhythm is also a great learning experience (especially if you can incorporate some hand clapping or other movements as well). A chant is a form of singing, after all. One textbook series I used had a rap by John DeMado for every unit.

I Can Play Musical Instruments

Some studies say that musical training correlates with language-learning skills: musicians are thought to be better at pronouncing the sounds and noticing the contrasts between sounds in the TL. Broca's area in the brain is very active in both learning a language and learning to play an instrument and, just as learning a second new language is easier after learning a first one, there is a similar crossover benefit between learning to play an instrument and learning a language.

ACTFL: Culture, all levels; **CEFR:** none

And then there's the entertainment value: students can not only showcase their linguistic skills, but also their musical prowess. There is an opportunity to incorporate TL culture as well. Ask my students who I've accompanied on my nose flute (an instrument from Africa) or who have played the goatskin drums purchased in Morocco. Other ways to add culture could be to play traditional pieces from TL composers and countries.

I Can Play a Sport

If you do a sport, by all means teach it to your students in the TL. Teach them how to swing a golf club, pitch a curve ball, or whatever you like to do. In college, I was on the fencing team and my students are fascinated with the equipment used, and all the French terms for it. I also have a *chistera* used in *pelota* (*jai alai* in Spanish) and enjoy sharing my interest in the sport when we learn about the Basque minority in France (and in the United States, also). All my students have had a chance to play French *pétanque* (somewhat like Italian bocce): we raised money to build a court at school, designed tee-shirts for our team, and invited area schools to competitions (with trophies).

> **ACTFL:** Culture, all levels; **CEFR:** A2

> **ACTFL:** Culture, all levels; **CEFR:** A2

But you don't need to be an athlete. I am a big fan of hockey, so we always do a unit on Quebec and factor in the sport. I can have my students find out which of our local hockey team are French Canadian (and at universities near us) and write them a note. Sometimes they answer! Then, we watch *The Rocket*, a hockey movie, and read a short story about hockey, *Le Chandail*, which also has a cartoon version we can watch.

> **ACTFL:** Interpretive (reading, watching) or Presentational (writing or speaking), all levels; **CEFR:** A2+ through B1+

The Olympic Games and March Madness are also offer chances to find the names of the athletes representing TL countries for various teams or sports, read their biographies, discuss their stats, follow their successes or losses, and even send them a message on social media; we have even gotten answers and, once, a video chat. We can also read the rules of play for a sport (my students had never heard of the luge before the Winter Olympics), learn names of various pieces of equipment or strategies used, and maybe become fans for life and/or impress their families with knowledge gained in your classroom.

I Can Play Video Games

The number of game-based sites just continues to increase: Class Tools https://ClassTools.net offers eight classic arcade games that can be made free of charge based on one vocabulary set. Other sites like Conjuguemos https://conjuguemos.com offers eight or more gamified activities to practice grammar and vocabulary. Kahoot, Quizizz, Quizlet Live, Blooket, and Gimkit are other sites where you can choose what and how students learn, practice, and review. Most of those educational game sites are not blocked at school. Chapter 8 has more information about using technology.

ACTFL: Interpretive, all levels; **CEFR:** A2+

What about the games the kids love to play? Try to find out if those are available to be played in the TL. Playing a game in the TL involves learning the names of things and some grammar rules for conversation during interactions; many will involve both listening and reading, with many repetitions. Some of my best students are gamers who play with others who speak the TL; my level 1 classes often contain several kids who are already comfortable with reading some French! Check out which popular games are available in the TL and perhaps consider adding game play (with a screenshot to prove it was done in the TL) as part of a choice board (see Chapter 11 for more about those). Some video games that can be played are (in Spanish) Rise of the Tomb Raider, Halo 3, Legend of Zelda, Dragon Age, Aura Kingdom; (in French) Assassin's Creed, Game of Thrones, Skyrim; (in German) Tomb Raider, Walking Dead, The Sims; (in Japanese) Legend of Zelda, Final Fantasy, and many more.

I Can Text

Texting is appropriate for use in communicating with students: my school uses Remind https://www.remind.com/ to offer reminders and updates for students (and parents), and the tech team makes me a Remind for each of my classes. PollEverywhere https://www.polleverywhere.com/ is fun to use to get feedback, give quizzes, or get quick responses to questions.

Why not use the ever-popular emojis to write a story for the students to read? I use Emojipedia https://emojipedia.org/ to write rebus stories (some words, some emojis that represent words or characters) and have students read them aloud, transcribe them into just words, or write some for me to read. Emojis are great for practicing vocabulary about emotions, also. You can use emojis on flashcards, too (a rocket for "space," for example) or challenge students to find good ones for you. One teacher I know has a cute "Know Me Through Emojis" slide show, where she introduces herself, likes and dislikes, and family to her students at the beginning of the year.

> **ACTFL:** Interpretive, all levels; **CEFR:** A1

Other Skills

There are so many other things you probably know how to do that could be used in your classroom. Can you act? Dress like a famous TL person and have students guess who you are. Draw? Write? Sharing a talent is a big part of social-emotional teaching and doing something you really enjoy will foster enthusiasm and enjoyment for you and your students.

What Special Events Do I Look Forward To?

Birthdays

Everybody loves a birthday! And every day is someone's – pick someone famous and celebrate theirs, yours, a pet's, or invent someone (or something) who has a birthday. In my level 2 classes, I do a unit on birthdays, first to review family vocabulary and how to describe a person (we say who we want to invite and why), then we create invitations (reviewing days, months, telling time), and then my students go online to select decorations, food, music, and games. This culminates in party proposals from small groups with the class voting on their favorite, and we have the winning party (or as close as I can get to it) in my classroom. Students are encouraged to bring a white elephant gift; they guess what might be in the package, and we can talk about objects, presents, and more. This makes it easier to keep in the TL for conversation.

> **ACTFL:** Interpretive (reading) Presentational (speaking); **CEFR:** B1+

Parties With Friends

This is a slightly different topic and different cultures have different practices. Find a snippet from a movie, or a music video with a party (mine particularly like Amir's *5 Minutes Avec Toi*) and compare to parties where you live. Practice talking about parties: plan a theme – the wackier the better – such as a baby gender reveal party, a wake for a "deceased" classroom object, a dinner in white in which everyone dresses up, a murder mystery party (everyone gets a character to play), and many others. On YouTube, there are videos in the TL with tips on how to plan a party. Talk, write, listen, and read about celebrity parties and events – and share your enthusiasm and interest. Better yet, let them plan a real party for you. Look at how to get a home ready for a party,

> **ACTFL:** Culture and comparisons, all levels; **CEFR:** A2+

> **ACTFL:** Presentational (planning), Interpretive (reading or video) Novice High and above; **CEFR:** A2+ or B1

what to wear to a party (including makeup), a music playlist (in the TL of course). Separate the class into groups and each can take one aspect of the party. Let them vote and talk about the results. There are SO many different aspects to use as inspiration for learning and using your language.

I am toying with the idea of describing a Mystery Party, giving daily clues about it, and asking students to guess what they think it might be.

Holidays and Vacations

Holidays are a great excuse for a party: learn TL traditions, decorations, foods, crafts, songs, dances, and dress. Go caroling to nearby schools, make a video for your pen pals about Halloween decorations and costumes in your town, read a book to elementary students on Read Across America Day. Every day is some sort of holiday (check Google and make daily slides to talk about International Cupcake Day or Talk Like a Pirate Day –

> **ACTFL:** Culture, all levels; **CEFR:** B1

in the TL of course). Use your enthusiasms: why celebrate your favorite holiday just once? Choose your favorite holiday and make it happen all year long in your classroom.

Vacations are called "holidays" by the British. Choose an exotic TL location – find airfare and other costs, somewhere to rent, activities to do (or not do). Role play checking into a hotel. Learn the future tense or the subjunctive (wishing). Use the past tense to share stories about vacations taken or things you have seen or done over break. Survey the class about the best honeymoon site they know – let your imagination guide you and your class on a new adventure.

Stop and Think

Stop and try at least one of these! Go back to your answers in the grid at the beginning of the chapter and see what you can come up with!

Sometimes the hardest part is not to find a topic, but to decide how to use it. Figure 3.3 is a list of activities/products you can refer to for inspiration.

Figure 3.3 Products

A
action plan
adventure
advertisement
advice column
album
anagram
analysis of samples
anecdote
animation
apparatus
artifact collection
audiotape recording
autobiography
anecdote
avatar
award

B
ballad
ballet
banner
biographical
  presentation
bio-poem
block picture story
blog
blueprints
book
book jacket
booklet
bookmark
book report
brainteaser
brochure
bullet chart
bulletin board
business letter

C
calendar
campaign speech

caption
card game
cartoon
CD cover
celebrity profile
ceramic
charade
chart
characterization
checklist
children's book
choral reading
cinquain
classified ad
clothing
collage
collection
comedy act
comic book
comment (blog)
commentary
commercial
comparison
computer program
conversation
costume
couplet
coupon
creative writing
critique
crossword puzzle

D
dance
debate
demonstration
description
design a structure
  new product
  new animal
diagram

dialogue
diary
dictionary entry
diorama
directions
discussion
display
documentary
dramatization
drawing

E
editorial
editorial cartoon
equipment
essay
etching
exaggeration
exhibit
explanation
eyewitness account

F
fabric
fairy tale
field trip
film
finger puppet(s)
flag
flannel board
flash cards
flip chart
flow chart
food
free verse
friendly letter
furniture

G
gadget
gallery
game

glossary
gossip column
graph
graphic organizer
greeting card
guidebook

H
haiku
hand puppet
handbook
handout
hat
headline
hieroglyphic
history
hypothesis

I
illustration
imprint
Instagram
instrument
interior monologue
interview
invention
invitation

J
jigsaw puzzle
jingle
job description
joke
journal

K
kite
kitsch

L
law
learning center
lecture

(Continued)

Figure 3.3 *(Continued)*

lesson plan
letter
letter of complaint
  opinion
  request
  support
  to editor
limerick
list
log
lyrics

M
machine
macramé
magazine article
manual
map
marionnette
mask
memorandum
mentor
metaphor
mime
mnemonic
mobile
mock trial
model
monologue
montage
monument
mosaic
movement
multimedia
mural
music
musical
myth

N
narration
needlework
newscast
newsletter
newspaper
newspaper ad
newspaper article
new story ending
notes
nursery rhyme

O
oath
observation
oral report
origami
order form
outline

P
painting
pamphlet
panel discussion
parody
pattern
pen pal letter
petition
photo essay
photograph
picture dictionary
pin page
  (Pinterest)
plan (house,
  travel)
planet description
play
playing cards
poem
political cartoon
postage stamp
post card
poster
prediction
press conference
prophecy
public service
  announcement
puppet show
puzzle

Q
quatrain
question
questionnaire
quilt
quiz

R
radio
  announcement
radio commercial

radio show
rap
rebus story
recipe
reply
report
reproduction
request
research report
resume
review
rewrite
rhyme
riddle
role-play
rubric

S
scenario
schedule
science fiction
  story
scrapbook
script
scroll
sculpture
seminar
series of letters
shopping list
short story
skit
sign
silk screen
simulation
slide show
slogan
soap opera
solution
solve a community
  problem
song
speech
stencil
stick puppet
story
storyboard
story problem
subject dictionary
survey
symbol

T
tall tale
telegram
teach a class
theory (formulate
  and defend)
time line
tools
toy
training session
translation
transparency
travel
  advertisement
travel log
TV newscast
Tweet
Twitter story

U
utopia (describe)

V
Venn diagram
verdict
videotape
visual aid
vocabulary list

W
wall hanging
wanted poster
warm-up
warrant for arrest
weather map
web
web page
WebQuest
woodcut
word game
word search
writing

X

Y
yearbook
  prediction

Z
zodiac chart
zoo map

Okay, it's time to list at least one creative idea about your current interests and talents that you had while reading this part of Chapter 3:

> **Unit topic:** _____ **Level** _____
> **I'm going to:** _____
> **Ways I can adapt this for other levels** (why not use this idea for ALL your classes?)

And now, let's talk about some more ways to make everyday things special in your classroom

Use the Familiar: Personalization

Getting inspiration and incorporating passions from daily life. Fill out this form.

I do this all the time, and like it:	1.
	2.
I had an interesting experience:	1.
	2.
My family's favorite traditions:	1.
	2.

Personalize Using Your Life Events
Use your own life (spouse or friend or children or pets) to inspire new classroom activities:

- Take your typical thing listed above and try to think of something to show/write/talk/read about or a song or work of art that goes with what you wrote above.
  - I do mindfulness with my students and have seen some amazing results (29% improvement in grades, for example).
  - I volunteer at a community food bank and found an article about this topic for my students to read (in France, les *Restos du Coeur*).

> **ACTFL:** Interpretive, all levels; **CEFR:** A2+

- Do you have any interesting or bizarre stories (meeting someone famous, trying something for the first time, an accident or embarrassment, etc.)? Telling those to your students

will not only be of high interest but will probably improve your relationship as your students will know you better.
- Every family has traditions. Which of yours could you use in a story (fiction or nonfiction), or actually do for a special day for students (maybe during high-stakes testing week or at semester end after they have taken the final?).

> **ACTFL:** Presentational, all levels; **CEFR:** B1

Here are a few examples of using my own daily life in the classroom: all activities were great for promoting basic conversational skills:

Why?

This is a game that my children inspired when they were toddlers. It seemed like almost every time I told them to do something, they would ask, "Why?" and keep asking it to forestall having to comply with my request. I made this into a game for my classroom: a student volunteer would make a statement such as "I like pizza." The class would chorus, "Why?" and the student would answer, "It's delicious." The class would keep asking "why," and we would keep track of how many

> **ACTFL:** Interpersonal, Intermediate Mid; **CEFR:** A2+ or B1

"whys" were answered before the student could not answer. Students would compete to see who could keep going the longest, and then the competition extended between classes, with high interest. Students spent time practicing and thinking in the TL to try to find statements that would hold up longer under questioning and would look up new vocabulary to use (and thereby teach it to the class). I served as dictionary and we also learned new vocabulary that way.

Hot Seat

When I was a college student overseas, I helped with English classes in a private high school. One day, the teacher was ill, and I was asked to fill in, all by myself. Lacking any lesson plans, I decided to let the students ask me anything they wanted to know about me and the United States. They fired questions at me relentlessly. This memory inspired me to create a similar situation in my classroom; every student must take a turn to be questioned and

> **ACTFL:** Interpersonal, Intermediate Mid; **CEFR:** B1+

must also ask a certain number of questions of other students. This is great for writing questions, listening and speaking skills (both for the questioner and the person being questioned), as well as social-emotional learning and teambuilding as we all get to know each other better.

Cognate Crush

This is an activity inspired by another overseas experience. I needed to make a copy of an audio recording and needed to purchase a cable to connect my device to another. Using a dictionary (Google didn't exist yet), I spent close to an hour composing and memorizing what I needed to say at the electronics store. When I looked up how to say "jack" all the dictionary supplied was the terms for the device to help in changing car tires, or the playing card, so my explanation was long: what one looked like (material, size, shape), the purpose it would be used for, etc. At the store, I launched into my memorized speech; the employee listened, nodding his head as I talked and talked, only to say, "Oh, un jack!" and I realized if I had just tried the English word first, I could have saved myself a lot of work! In this activity, I give students a variety of readings (scientific articles, an installation manual, and an operation guide from devices I purchased, some current events about the environment, politics, etc.) and they are asked to locate and post cognates on a Padlet board for the students to read. Then I asked the students, with a partner, to write something using as many of those cognates as possible (with bonus points for whoever uses the most in a believable context). I converted the winning story into a rebus (pictures replacing words) for the whole class to read as practice.

> **ACTFL:** Interpretive (reading)
> Presentational (writing) Novice Mid;
> **CEFR:** A1 (reading) B1 (writing)

Personalize Using Students' Lives

One thing I like to do is to use student names on worksheets and quizzes. It takes longer than just using the ones provided, but it's worth it when they read and comment on the sentences their names are in. This also helps me get to know their names faster.

After your share your interesting or scary true story; have students each tell you one (in a survey or other written form, or as a speaking activity).

> **ACTFL:** Presentational, Advanced Low;
> **CEFR:** B1

It is always rather fun to do a survey either before or after a break (summer or a holiday) and make a "Find Someone Who" sheet for them to circulate and find the person who did or plans to do these things.

> **ACTFL:** Interpersonal, Novice Mid and above; **CEFR:** A1

Survey your students at the beginning of the year: favorite singer, actor, actress, superhero, whatever, and work those into stories.

Use students' skills and have a talent show; I have my students either exhibit a talent or be the announcer/describer for a friend who has a talent.

Never

For this activity I give all students the same number of dried beans, and we all sit in a circle. Using a metal can, we take turns telling something we have never done (good negative preterit tense practice). Everyone who HAS done that thing must drop a bean into the can (it makes a nice, satisfying loud sound) and say where or with whom or when. When the can has gone round the circle, the person to the speaker's left starts it again with a new personal statement. I reward the "least experienced" (last one left) as well as "most experienced" (first to run out of beans).

> **ACTFL:** Presentational and Interpretive, Intermediate Mid; **CEFR:** A2

Personalize on a Broader Level

Current, local, national, or international events are also things to consider as a springboard for your imagination. Don't forget ongoing topics such as health trends, the environment, national elections, and other news making events in TL countries, etc. For advice on how to find such information, see the section on technology in Chapter 8.

> **ACTFL:** Culture practices and perspectives, Novice High and above; **CEFR:** B1

REFLECTION TIME: Personalization ideas

What I'd like to try first: _____

What would I need to do this? _____

Who else would be involved (practice, support)? _____

How much time will this take? _____

4

Imagination and Creativity

Introduction

Using your imagination instead of just your personal experiences can add a great new dimension to your teaching. Borrow some ideas from industrial think tanks (like synectics), little quirks of the target language (TL) being studied, or stand-up comics techniques to get a laugh. Humor is great for the soul (and the classroom) and has been shown to stimulate long-term retention. Try these and you will not be disappointed!

Flights of Fancy

Synectics

One of my favorite activities to stimulate creative thinking is synectics, which I learned about when our school was changing to a block schedule, and we were investigating new strategies. This is usually done as a whole-class activity, but it is also quite possible to do with a partner or even alone; I do it all by myself when searching for a creative way to describe something.

Step 1 is to describe the object/person/idea: "you are a [fill in the topic]. How do you look and feel?" Write down your ideas. (If you can get someone else to help with this, groups are often more creative than individuals.) Example: describe the main character in a book. [List of words is generated.]

Step 2 is to make analogies using a different object/person/idea. "If someone/something with [words on the list] were a [pick any topic: fruit/animal/machine/etc.], what kind would it/s/he be?" and again write down your ideas. Choose the strangest or most "creative" thing from that list.

Step 3 is to reuse Step 1: you are a (whatever you chose in step two, for example, a telescope), how do you look/feel? Again, record the ideas – the looks, emotions, typical activities, etc.

Step 4 looks for compressed conflict. See if two items on the list from Step 3 can form an oxymoron (almost opposites), or take a really good word from the list and pair it with its opposite.

Step 5: reuse Step 2. What type of plant (or other categories like animal, food, household object, etc.) is best described by [oxymoron you chose in Step 4].

Step 6: put the starting topic and the result from Step 5 together – now you have a truly creative pairing that should spark some unusual connections and ideas when you ask the question "How is X like Y?" How is taking a photo like baking chocolate chip cookies? How is a puppy like a Ferrari? Use these flights of fancy to generate a picture, and create a story, poem, song, or cartoon (use your imagination) inspired by the image.

Idioms

The phrase "flights of fancy" is an idiom. An idiom is a group of words whose meaning cannot be deduced from the individual words; I think of an idiom as somewhat poetic, or at least easy to illustrate. Buy a book such as *Edible French,* by Clotilde Dusoulier of the blog *Chocolate and Zucchini*, on idioms involving food. There are many, many idioms for every TL. Why not use TL idioms for teaching?

> **ACTFL:** Culture, Novice High and above;
> **CEFR:** A1 through B2

- You can use some to compare/contrast with those in our language (we say "raining cats and dogs" and the French say "raining ropes" and in Spain I heard *llover chuzos* "raining sharp sticks") or find some that don't exist in our language. Illustrate them and have students write them in the TL and guess the equivalent in English, or have students illustrate them as posters.

- Give a "bravo" point each time students manage to work one into a conversation or composition.
- Teach them to students as a call-and-response signal to start class, end an activity, etc. (Example in English: teacher says "See you later" and students respond "alligator").

Humor

Humor is possibly the very best teaching strategy of all. Using humor in the classroom contributes to a positive learning atmosphere by reducing tensions and making more amicable student-teacher relationships. It also keeps students interested and motivated. In addition, humor helps less sociable students feel part of the class/peer group and they are then more likely to join in communicative activities. Brain research also shows that using humor and laughter increases retention. It also stimulates both creative and critical thinking.

You know the standard silliness that appeals to children of any age: anything bathroom-oriented, silly accidents (like slipping on a banana peel), sounds like "yum" or burps, silly curse words (geez Louise, dadgummit, etc.). Find what those are in the TL culture and insert those occasionally in lessons, stories, etc. Whenever possible, try to look for something humorous in any situation, and if it's not there, add it.

Don't forget to insert humor in a worksheet, test, or quiz. Put in celebrity names, teachers' or students' names, silly geographical (the name of your town or school) or cultural references, or current ("What is the Little Prince's favorite free time occupation? Listening to Prince's music.").

Don't overlook the usefulness of a good "Dad joke," riddle, or pun. Translate from English into your TL and have fun!

Internet as Inspiration

If you find something interesting or entertaining, use it in the classroom; students will like it, too.

- A couple of years ago, I discovered the popular Internet "shame" photos where pets were photographed with a sign (around their neck or nearby) saying what their transgression was: I ate the birthday cake, peed on the hamster, etc. I said to myself: my students are studying the past tense – how fun would it

ACTFL: Presentational, Intermediate Mid and above; **CEFR:** A2+

- be to post (on a private Padlet or Flipgrid or Jamboard) a "shame photo" for a classmate with an outlandish but funny reason for them to be ashamed? It was a big hit.
- Search for "epic fail" photos or videos to illustrate vocabulary. I have some funny ones of people illustrating various ways not to walk, bake something, serve a tennis ball, etc.
- Memes are easy to make. I moderated the meme contributions to "Manie Musicale 2022," a March-Madness-style bracket activity that paired current music videos against each other, on which students voted. We challenged students to make memes about their favorite videos, and thousands poured in. Memes can be quite clever; a photo is paired with a short written text. Choose a photo of someone or something the students enjoy and add a comment for everyone's entertainment. I have some favorite memes made into posters for my classroom, too. Have your students help make memes and host your own contest.

  ACTFL: Presentational, Intermediate Low and above; **CEFR:** A2

- The Internet is also great for finding fun visuals. I made signs for my classroom, for example, a picture of a stamp and stamp pad. The stamp says "WTF?" and my sign subtitles that as, "Was That French?" We use the site *Awkward Family Photos* https://awkwardfamilyphotos.com/ to talk about families and practice describing people. I made a slide show of mug shots of people who were arrested, from police sources online, to practice describing people. For clothing (make sure you preview first!) try *People of Walmart* https://www.peopleofwalmart.com/ for some pretty outrageous outfits and hair styles. There are also some really unusual prom outfits posted online too.
- Silly songs and activities are also easy to find through colleagues or just by surfing YouTube or social media. I use *Simon's Cat* videos, *Just Dance* French videos (as brain breaks), and humorous commercials (especially those in the Noel Madness series each year).
- Blooper videos are great. Why not make a blooper video or cartoon (see Chapter 8 for some suggestions of sites for making these) of common mistakes in the TL? These could be grammar errors (especially gender) or vocabulary failures (such as announcing you are pregnant instead of saying you are embarrassed) or breaking cultural rules (such as using the wrong form of address, incorrect table manner, giving an inappropriate gift, etc.). My students always remember these stories.

Strategies from Stand-up Comedians

Surprise

One common strategy in humor is to combine things that don't normally go together. As an example, I created sentences for a unit on daily activities using the vocabulary in unusual ways: I am going to iron the lawn, wash the trash, dust the toothbrush, etc., and then I challenged students to write and sketch a similar statement. Then, using only their illustrations, we tried to use the image to guess and reconstruct the sentence.

> **ACTFL:** Presentational, Novice High and above; **CEFR:** A2

Exaggeration

Overreact to everything! I cannot draw even a stick figure well, but when I have truly failed at trying to draw one, I point at it and exclaim what a great artist I am and how this should hang in a museum. Have the kids ooh and aah at your "masterpiece."

Numbers are also fun. Set up a story where a small number (of items, money, people) is expected, and then say "only" and a huge number. Or, set it up where a big number is expected, and say "It's a huge amount" first, and then a tiny number. Example: "I went shopping for school supplies and I found a really cool pencil. It only cost ten thousand dollars. It looked like a unicorn and would write only in Italian [get silly with your description!]. An unbelievably huge number of women tried to fight me for it because I got the last one, but I punched one in the arm and the other screamed and both of them let go of the pencil!"

Rule of Three

Begin by making a statement about a category. Then list examples in threes, with the first two normal, and the third one unexpected, such as "We are going to learn a lot about (the TL) this year: culture, conversation, and some other stuff that starts with a c."

Keep it Real

True stories with humorous elements are much better than invented stories. You have a phone; if something funny happens or you think of a funny story about yourself or someone else, make a note in your phone and figure out a good unit or class to tell that story.

The idea(s) that I'd like to try FIRST: _____
_____

What topic(s) can I use this for? _____
_____

Preliminary Chapter 5-Additional Information on Organization of Capsules

Goal Setting, Innovation, and *Implementation Capsules*

Introduction

To facilitate the implementation of creativity, goal setting, innovation, and implementation, we have included a total of 33 **capsules in Chapters 5, 6, and 7**: 11 capsules in Chapter 5, 13 capsules in Chapter 6, and nine capsules in Chapter 7.

Jump aboard one of the space capsules in Chapters 5-Modes of Instruction, 6-Teaching Ideas and 7-Promotional Ideas to enjoy a fun and exciting adventure that you create and direct! Chapter 5's capsules discuss modes of instruction, Chapter 6's show new teaching ideas, and Chapter 7's capsules offer promotional ideas for world language classes.

Each capsule contains portions of the six steps to success at being creative: a touch of curiosity, a dash of imagination, creativity, goal setting, implementation, and evaluation. Follow some easy-to-use guides while you direct adventures that allow your creativity to flourish!

There are four steps to follow with each capsule: **Getting Started, For Your Consideration, Time to Brainstorm,** and **Call to Action**. Most and best of all: HAVE FUN on your adventure!

Each space capsule page can be photocopied and kept in a binder and could be used just for you or as a departmental activity.

DOI: 10.4324/9781003293255-5

Also: dare to make your **own** space capsules. Use the categories and capsules from the book, but also feel free to add your own to the mix. You may also change those used in this chapter to suit your own personal needs. We have provided space to make notes on each capsule, and a page at the end of this chapter that allows you to make your own Goal Setting/Innovation/Implementation Capsules.

ACTFL Standards/Communication/Proficiency Levels

All the capsules in this chapter – lesson plans, creative starters, recipes, etc. – can be used at any level of the ACTFL and CEFR standards described in the Preface to this book on pages xvi and xvii. In fact, one creative idea can, by varying the difficulty of tasks, be used for all classes, no matter what level!

In this book, TL stands for the target language that you teach.

Enjoy your adventure into the creativity sphere!

5

Modes of Instruction
Goal Setting, Innovation, and Implementation Capsules

Introduction

This chapter offers 11 space capsules* with different modes of instruction. Choose different modes to try out as the school year progresses. Put on your creativity and positivity hat for the journey. Toast to your creativity and positivity! Some of the modes of instruction include comprehensible input (CI), teaching proficiency through reading and storytelling (TPRS), multiple intelligences, differentiated instruction, cooperative learning, and more. Take risks, have fun, and show and share your creativity and positivity. Variety is the spice of life!

*Please refer to the Detailed Table of Contents to view a list of each of the 11 modes of instruction space capsules.

CAPSULE 1 – LESSON PLANNING

GETTING STARTED: *Questions to answer*

1. Why change your lesson plans?
2. What are you going to change?
3. When are you going to make the changes?
4. How are you going to do this? **(BE CURIOUS, IMAGINE, CREATE!)**
5. What results do you expect?
6. What are some problems you could have?
7. How will you know if it is successful?
8. What positivity could result from this?

FOR YOUR CONSIDERATION

1. Change teaching strategies: Think about trying/using CI, TPRS, multiple intelligences, differentiated instruction, or more technology. How about active student learning, student-centered, pair work, small groups, peer teaching, or student teams? Try a variety of teaching strategies throughout the year!
2. Use more hands-on materials, skits, and fun activities.
3. Make a new lesson plan each week. Make changes as needed. **BE FLEXIBLE!**

TIME TO BRAINSTORM

1. Do an online search – current teaching strategies for world languages.
2. Visit the ACTFL website to learn more about the proficiency levels and can-do statements.
3. Speak with another world language colleague. Share your lesson plan ideas with her/him/them and vice versa.
4. Consult with the department head and share ideas about lesson planning.
5. Ask the students what activities they would like to do in class.
6. Is this new lesson plan imaginative?

Copyright material from Deborah Blaz and Tom Alsop (2023), *Sparking Creativity in the World Language Classroom: Strategies and Ideas to Build Your Students' Language Skills,* Routledge.

CALL TO ACTION

1. Select a date to change your lesson plans.
2. Gather any materials you will need.
3. Announce and celebrate your new plans.
4. **Then, DO IT!**
5. Make a results chart to track progress.
6. List what worked and what did not.
7. Accept very good results, make new resolutions (and notes on what went well), and then revel in the creativity from making the changes!

The idea(s) on this page that I'd like to try FIRST:

_____
_____

The first thing I need to do to implement this is: _____

How did things go? What worked well? Why?

_____
_____

Will I use these ideas again in the future? What changes are needed?

_____

Copyright material from Deborah Blaz and Tom Alsop (2023), *Sparking Creativity in the World Language Classroom: Strategies and Ideas to Build Your Students' Language Skills,* Routledge.

CAPSULE 2 – SEATING ARRANGEMENTS

GETTING STARTED

1. Why change your seating arrangements/charts?
2. What are you going to change?
3. Set a date for the changes.
4. Will the change be extreme?
5. How will you do this? **(BE CURIOUS, IMAGINE, CREATE!)**
6. What are some problems you could have?
7. How could your new seating chart improve the learning environment?

FOR YOUR CONSIDERATION

1. Seats in a circle.
2. Seats in a horseshoe.
3. Seats in pairs.
4. Seats in groups of three.
5. Seats in groups of four.
6. Seats in groups of six.
7. Seats in a square.
8. Change your seating chart regularly (i.e., every two months). **BE FLEXIBLE!**

TIME TO BRAINSTORM

1. Do an on-line search to find popular seating arrangements in schools. Why are they good?
2. Speak with a colleague and ask about their favorite seating arrangements. These teachers can also be in other disciplines.
3. Speak with heads of departments and ask them about their favorite seating arrangements.
4. Ask the students about their favorite seating arrangements!
5. Imagine a totally novel seating chart.

CALL TO ACTION

1. Set a date to begin.
2. Draw your seating chart/arrangement – use a computer program, if possible.
3. Contemplate the change and envision the creativity and imagination in the change you are using.
4. **DO IT!**
5. Keep a diary with results of the new seating arrangement.
6. **CELEBRATE** the **NEW**! Enthusiasm is catching with students!

The idea(s) on this page that I'd like to try FIRST:
_____
_____

The first thing I need to do to implement this is: _____

How did things go? What worked well? Why?
_____
_____

Will I use these ideas again in the future? What changes are needed?
_____

CAPSULE 3 – COMPREHENSIBLE INPUT (CI)

GETTING STARTED

1. Why change to CI teaching strategy?
2. Set a date for the changes.
3. How will you do this?
4. What will be some obstacles to overcome?
5. Will using CI improve the student-learning of the TL?
6. How can you make the use of CI as a powerful creative tool? **BE FLEXIBLE!**

FOR YOUR CONSIDERATION

1. Hand out a sheet, or send digitally, to students with everyday TL words you will use all the time in class.
2. Try to speak 90% TL with your students.
3. Use mini stories for practice. **(BE CURIOUS, IMAGINE, CREATE!)**
4. Explain basic vocabulary and grammar by speaking only in your TL.
5. Ask students questions in the TL and have them answer in the TL.

> **ACTFL:** Interpersonal, all levels; **CEFR:** A1

6. Have them ask you questions in the TL.

> **ACTFL:** Interpersonal, all levels; **CEFR:** A1

7. Use CI throughout the year. If unable to use CI all the time, mix it with some of your own tried-and-true strategies.

TIME TO BRAINSTORM

1. Do a search online and find out how to use CI. Be sure to look up the experts in CI.
2. Speak with a colleague who uses CI. Ask her/him/them about successes, failures, and helpful tips.

Copyright material from Deborah Blaz and Tom Alsop (2023), *Sparking Creativity in the World Language Classroom: Strategies and Ideas to Build Your Students' Language Skills*, Routledge.

3. Speak with heads of departments and ask them about their favorite CI teaching and learning activities.
4. How will you prepare students to try the CI method of world-language learning?
5. Imagine and invent some fun learning games for students to read, write, speak, and listen only in the TL.

CALL TO ACTION

1. Celebrate your decision to use CI with your colleagues.
2. Use a class roster to record each day when students speak only in the TL.
3. Encourage your students to speak only in the TL.
4. **DO IT!**
5. Award extra credit or world language stickers to students who speak only in their TL.
6. Toast to your IMAGINATION. Then take notes to make it even better next time!

The idea(s) on this page that I'd like to try FIRST:

_____

_____

The first thing I need to do to implement this is: _____

How did things go? What worked well? Why?

_____

_____

Will I use these ideas again in the future? What changes are needed?

_____

CAPSULE 4 – TPRS (TEACHING PROFICIENCY THROUGH READING AND STORYTELLING)

GETTING STARTED

1. Why do TPRS? What do you want your students to do with TPRS?
2. Do an online search and find information on TPRS and how to implement it in class.
3. When will you start?
4. How will you do this? **BE FLEXIBLE!**
5. What readers will you use? Other materials? Digital materials?
6. Will you teach grammar concepts? How?
7. What strategies can you use to keep all in the TL? **(BE CURIOUS, IMAGINE, CREATE!)**

FOR YOUR CONSIDERATION

1. Hand out, or send digitally, a list to students with everyday TL words you will use every day in class. Have students practice them until learned.
2. Speak only in the TL with your students.
3. Use short novels and books of short stories in your TL.

> **ACTFL:** Presentational, Novice Mid and above; **CEFR:** A2+

4. Let students re-tell what they read in the TL.

> **ACTFL:** Interpersonal, Novice Mid and above; **CEFR:** A1 and above

5. Ask students questions about readings in the TL.

> **ACTFL:** Presentational, Intermediate Low and above; **CEFR:** A2+

6. Have a reader's theater and let the students act out what they read.
7. Use TPRS throughout the year. Mix TPRS into some of your own activities.

Copyright material from Deborah Blaz and Tom Alsop (2023), *Sparking Creativity in the World Language Classroom: Strategies and Ideas to Build Your Students' Language Skills,* Routledge.

TIME TO BRAINSTORM

1. Speak with a colleague who uses TPRS. Share ideas. What works for her/him/them?
2. Go online and look up the experts on TPRS. Send them an e-mail and tell them what you are doing.
3. Speak with colleagues in other schools and ask them what their favorite TPRS teaching techniques are.
4. Get comments from students shortly after you start your readings with them.
5. Imagine and invent some of your own super-creative ideas to use with TPRS.

CALL TO ACTION

1. **DO IT!**
2. Celebrate students' successes after reading your first book. Have a little party!
3. Ask students to use their new listening and speaking skills to do a TV commercial in the TL about a book you just read.
4. Award prizes to the top ten readers in your class.
5. Invite your department head to watch one of your successful classes in action!
6. Have a special Parents Day and ask the parents to visit two of your best classes. Show off their reading and speaking skills.

ACTFL: Presentational, Intermediate Mid;
CEFR: B1

The idea(s) on this page that I'd like to try FIRST:
_____
_____

The first thing I need to do to implement this is: _____

How did things go? What worked well? Why?
_____

Will I use these ideas again in the future? What changes are needed?
_____

Copyright material from Deborah Blaz and Tom Alsop (2023), *Sparking Creativity in the World Language Classroom: Strategies and Ideas to Build Your Students' Language Skills,* Routledge.

CAPSULE 5 – MULTIPLE INTELLIGENCES

GETTING STARTED

1. Why try doing multiple intelligences?
2. Do an online search about strategies to teach about learning preferences in a world language class.
3. What are you going to do? **(BE CURIOUS, IMAGINE, CREATE!)**
4. How or what can you teach using multiple intelligences?
5. What results do you expect?
6. Do you need to gather materials to do this? **(BE FLEXIBLE!)**

FOR YOUR CONSIDERATION

> **ACTFL:** Interpretive, Novice Mid and above; **CEFR:** A2

> **ACTFL:** Presentational, Novice High and above; **CEFR:** B1

1. Think about using learning stations (centers). Have a learning station activity for each of these: sports, music, dance, food, video, holidays, monuments, celebrities, etc.
2. Have students work in teams as they visit the stations. Have a captain for each team.
3. Have follow-up reports from each team on their favorite stations.
4. Play music in the background during the Multiple Intelligence Day.
5. You may want to do it several times throughout the year for creative enrichment. You can choose to do each session for one week at a time.

TIME TO BRAINSTORM!

1. Go online and get information on Howard Gardner and multiple intelligences.
2. Speak with colleagues in your district or others who have used learning preferences in lesson plans.

Copyright material from Deborah Blaz and Tom Alsop (2023), *Sparking Creativity in the World Language Classroom: Strategies and Ideas to Build Your Students' Language Skills*, Routledge.

3. Invite a colleague or an administrator to watch your class in action as they do work involving learning preferences.
4. Ask the students what activities they would like to do in class.
5. Imagine how else you can use these in your classroom.

CALL TO ACTION

1. **DO IT!**
2. Have students make signs announcing Multiple Intelligences Week.
3. Award special prizes to the most creative students.
4. Celebrate your successes with your colleagues. Go out after school to your favorite pub.
5. Ask your students to plan a future lesson using multiple intelligences.
6. Invite a colleague to help you plan your next multiple intelligences extravaganza.
7. How did it go?
8. **CELEBRATE CREATIVITY!** Have the class prepare some food for their help in making this endeavor a truly imaginative and unforgettable moment!

The idea(s) on this page that I'd like to try FIRST:

_____

_____

The first thing I need to do to implement this is: _____

How did things go? What worked well? Why?

_____

_____

Will I use these ideas again in the future? What changes are needed?

_____

CAPSULE 6 – DIFFERENTIATED INSTRUCTION

GETTING STARTED

1. Why try doing differentiated instruction?
2. Do an online search about strategies to teach differentiated instruction in world language classes. Do a search and find information books by Deborah Blaz on differentiated instruction.
3. What are you going to do to set-up differentiated instruction in your classroom?
4. How do you plan to get differentiated instruction started?
5. What materials will you need?

FOR YOUR CONSIDERATION

1. Think about doing learning stations (centers) and/or choice learning as well.
2. Know your learners' interests. Have a learning station for each of their interests.

ACTFL: Interpretive, Novice Mid and above; **CEFR:** A2

3. You may also include stations in vocabulary and grammar. Put out materials at each station. **(BE CURIOUS, IMAGINE, CREATE!)**
4. Have students work in teams as they visit the stations. Have a captain for each team.
5. See differences and similarities between learners' interests and styles of learning.
6. Accept your role as teacher-facilitator. **(BE FLEXIBLE!)**

TIME TO BRAINSTORM

1. Applaud the active learning going on now. Applaud your students. Be a cheerleader!
2. Speak with colleagues in your district or others who have some expertise in using differentiated instruction in their classrooms.

Copyright material from Deborah Blaz and Tom Alsop (2023), *Sparking Creativity in the World Language Classroom: Strategies and Ideas to Build Your Students' Language Skills,* Routledge.

3. Invite a colleague to watch your class in action as they visit their learning centers.
4. Invite an administrator to watch your students in action.
5. Ask the students what activities they would like to do in class.
6. **IMAGINE** how else you can use differentiated instruction in your classroom.

CALL TO ACTION

1. **DO IT!**
2. Celebrate your students' successes. Award certificates to all, but offer special prizes to the most creative students! (See Chapter 10.)
3. Celebrate your successes with your colleagues. See Chapter 10 for more on celebrations.
4. Invite a colleague to help you plan your next differentiated instruction extravaganza.
5. How did it go? Take notes on what will make it even better next time.
6. DECORATE with creativity. Create posters about your differentiated instruction experience and decorate the room with the best ones. If using iPads/tablets or laptops, make digital posters.

The idea(s) on this page that I'd like to try FIRST:

_____
_____

The first thing I need to do to implement this is: _____

How did things go? What worked well? Why?

_____
_____

Will I use these ideas again in the future? What changes are needed?

_____

CAPSULE 7 – COOPERATIVE LEARNING

GETTING STARTED

1. What is cooperative learning? Why do students work for a common goal?
2. Do an online search and find information on cooperative learning and how to implement it.
3. What do you want your students to learn in cooperative groups? Vocabulary, grammar, culture? Practice reading and speaking? Consider doing a culture project.
4. When will you start?
5. How will you do this? Will you use learning stations, multiple intelligences, heterogenous, or homogenous groups?
6. What materials will you use? Digital materials? How many students in each group?
7. Will you be the primary facilitator? Will you have student facilitators? New seating charts?
8. What strategies can you use to keep all in the TL?
9. Have each cooperative group choose a fun name their group. **(BE FLEXIBLE!)**

FOR YOUR CONSIDERATION

1. Hand out, or send digitally, a sheet to students with a brief explanation of your goals in using cooperative learning.
2. Speak only in the TL with your students.
3. Use a variety of materials: readers, grammar books, vocabulary guides, etc.
4. Choose a captain for each group. Assign each group member a task.
5. Encourage students to ask you and each other questions. You are the facilitator!
6. How will you grade students' work? A global grade for each group? A grade for each student?
7. Prepare an assessment form for your grading.

TIME TO BRAINSTORM

1. Speak with a colleague who has used cooperative learning with her/his/their classes. Share ideas: what works for her/him/them?
2. Award prizes to the best workers in each cooperative group.
3. Speak with colleagues in other schools and ask them what their favorite strategies are to incorporate cooperative learning in class.
4. Get comments from students. Have them evaluate their cooperative group.
5. **(BE CURIOUS, IMAGINE, CREATE!)** Imagine and invent some of your own super-creative ideas to use with cooperative learning.

CALL TO ACTION

1. **DO IT!**
2. Celebrate the success of the cooperative classes: a night without homework? A food party? A video?
3. Ask students to invite their parents to visit and watch your cooperative groups in action!
4. Award prizes to the best cooperative group, to the most improved group, and/or the most creative cooperative group.
5. Invite your principal and department head to watch your cooperative groups in action!

The idea(s) on this page that I'd like to try FIRST:

_____

_____

The first thing I need to do to implement this is: _____

How did things go? What worked well? Why?

_____

_____

Will I use these ideas again in the future? What changes are needed?

_____

Copyright material from Deborah Blaz and Tom Alsop (2023), *Sparking Creativity in the World Language Classroom: Strategies and Ideas to Build Your Students' Language Skills*, Routledge.

CAPSULE 8 – PEER TEACHING

GETTING STARTED

1. Why should I try peer teaching?
2. Do an online search about strategies for using peer teaching in world language classes.
3. What do you want to accomplish?
4. What do you need to do to prepare? **(BE CURIOUS, IMAGINE, CREATE!)**
5. What results do you expect?
6. How can you accomplish using peer teaching in your TL classes? **(BE FLEXIBLE!)**

FOR YOUR CONSIDERATION

1. Aristotle said: "To teach is to learn twice." Select a top student in each class to teach a segment of class. This can be about vocabulary, grammar, culture, a song, a recipe, a dance, etc.
2. Divide the class into small groups. Appoint the top student in each group to be the teacher for a day. Give her/him/them any needed materials and let them know what you want them to teach.
3. Have special awards for the best peer teacher.
4. Have students evaluate their groups (what did they learn?).
5. Video the groups or teachers.
6. Play music in the background while students work.

TIME TO BRAINSTORM

1. Speak with colleagues in your school and other schools who have done peer teaching.
2. Meet with students who will be peer teachers after class or after school. Help them prepare.
3. Invite a colleague to watch your class in action as they use peer teaching.
4. Invite your principal to watch your teacher-groups in action.

Copyright material from Deborah Blaz and Tom Alsop (2023), *Sparking Creativity in the World Language Classroom: Strategies and Ideas to Build Your Students' Language Skills*, Routledge.

5. Imagine what else you can do with peer teaching.
6. Have an assessment tool to evaluate your students' work. Give all students a grade for their work.

CALL TO ACTION

1. Announce who the peer teachers will be. Explain to the peer teachers why they were selected.
2. **DO IT!**
3. Award special prizes to the most creative students.
4. Have a peer teacher party. Prepare native dishes, watch a movie, have fun!
5. Ask your students to plan a future lesson using peer teachers in the plans.
6. Invite a colleague to work with you the next time you use peer teachers.
7. How did it go? Have students evaluate what happened.
8. **CELEBRATE CREATIVITY!** Have students create a TV commercial about peer teaching. They can mention its good points. Do all in your TL. Record a video!

The idea(s) on this page that I'd like to try FIRST:
_____
_____

The first thing I need to do to implement this is: _____

How did things go? What worked well? Why?
_____
_____

Will I use these ideas again in the future? What changes are needed?
_____

Copyright material from Deborah Blaz and Tom Alsop (2023), *Sparking Creativity in the World Language Classroom: Strategies and Ideas to Build Your Students' Language Skills*, Routledge.

CAPSULE 9 – TEAM TEACHING

GETTING STARTED

1. Why should I try team teaching?
2. Do an online search about strategies for using team teaching in world language classes.
3. What are your goals? When and how will you do team teaching? Why do team teaching?
4. What do you need to do to prepare? **(BE CURIOUS, IMAGINE, CREATE!)**
5. What results do you expect?
6. How can I accomplish my goals using team teaching in my world-language classes? **(BE FLEXIBLE!)**

FOR YOUR CONSIDERATION

1. Select a teacher in your department who teaches the same world language, level, and meeting time as you. Invite her/him/them to try team teaching one lesson with you.
2. Meet with the person who has agreed to team teach with you and pick topics/pages to team teach. One of you might do vocabulary, the other grammar.
3. Be a facilitator and walk about the class while the other presents. Take turns.
4. Video all.
5. If you want to get really daring, invite an English teacher and team teach a chapter on Ernest Hemingway (for Spanish-English students), a famous French painter, a famous German musician (team with a music teacher), or a Chinese scientist.

TIME TO BRAINSTORM

1. Find out if anyone in your school (teacher or administrator) has ever team taught. If so, speak with them for teaching tips.
2. Invite an administrator to watch your team-teaching event.
3. Did you meet your goals? What were your successes?

Copyright material from Deborah Blaz and Tom Alsop (2023), *Sparking Creativity in the World Language Classroom: Strategies and Ideas to Build Your Students' Language Skills,* Routledge.

4. Speak with your students afterward. Did they enjoy the team teaching? Why or why not?
5. Have an assessment tool to evaluate your students' work. Give all students a grade for their work.

CALL TO ACTION

1. **DO IT!**
2. Ask your students to plan a future lesson plan in another discipline for you and your teaching colleague in the other discipline. It could be a math teacher, science teacher, social studies teacher, physical education teacher, or a family consumer science teacher.
3. Get both classes – your world language class and the other discipline – to prepare an interdisciplinary unit.
4. **CELEBRATE CREATIVITY**! Have both classes prepare a special sweet or candy to toast the success.
5. Invite parents to visit the team teaching classes to witness a display of **PURE CREATIVITY!**
6. **RISK TAKE:** Do a special world language lecture class for students in all languages of a given level. Meet once a week at the same time and have three or four language teachers share the planning. You will need a large room. You could also team teach and do a chapter on vocabulary with two world language classes.

The idea(s) on this page that I'd like to try FIRST:
_____
_____

The first thing I need to do to implement this is: _____

How did things go? What worked well? Why?
_____
_____

Will I use these ideas again in the future? What changes are needed?
_____

Copyright material from Deborah Blaz and Tom Alsop (2023), *Sparking Creativity in the World Language Classroom: Strategies and Ideas to Build Your Students' Language Skills,* Routledge.

CAPSULE 10 – LEARNING STATIONS

GETTING STARTED

1. Why do learning stations? Students can do fun activities – vocabulary, grammar worksheets, listen to and watch video clips, do a culture project, read, write, and speak.
2. Do an online search about strategies to use learning stations in your classroom?
3. How do you plan to do learning stations? **(BE CURIOUS, IMAGINE, CREATE!)**
4. What materials will you need? How long will it take?

FOR YOUR CONSIDERATION

1. Think about using learning stations (centers) with differentiated instruction, and/or multiple intelligences. What ACTL standard(s) will be addressed?
2. Know your learners' interests. Arrange seats in a semi-circle with four to six students in a group. Have four or five stations with one for vocabulary exercises/activities, one for grammar tasks, one for culture tasks/assignments, one for listening/speaking activities, and a final one for reading and writing.
3. Identify differences and similarities between learners' interests and styles of learning.
4. Have easy-to-use directions for students to follow at each station. Decide on how much time students should spend at each station. Will you use learning stations for more than one day? Do students have to do every station?
5. What student assessment will you use? Will there be an individual or group grade? Make things easy to grade.
6. Accept your role as teacher facilitator. **(BE FLEXIBLE!)**
7. **DO IT!**

TIME TO BRAINSTORM

1. **Applaud the active student-centered learning** going on while students use their stations to learn.

Copyright material from Deborah Blaz and Tom Alsop (2023), *Sparking Creativity in the World Language Classroom: Strategies and Ideas to Build Your Students' Language Skills,* Routledge.

2. Speak with colleagues in your district or others who have some expertise in using learning stations in their classrooms.
3. Invent an **easy-to-use** grading scale for this teaching strategy.
4. Invite an administrator to watch your class in action.
5. Imagine other creative ideas to include during learning stations in your classroom. Take pictures and/or video of your students working. Share those with the class!
6. Get student reactions to the learning stations.
7. Invite parents to visit and see the learning stations in action.

CALL TO ACTION

1. **DO IT!**
2. **CELEBRATE!** Celebrate your students' successes. Award certificates of creativity to all.
3. Award special prizes to the most creative students (stickers, candy, fake money).
4. Present a professional development session to your world language department of your school about using learning stations.
5. Make an announcement over the public address (PA) system about the success of the learning stations.
6. Place a write-up in your school paper or school website about your learning stations!

The idea(s) on this page that I'd like to try FIRST:
_____
_____

The first thing I need to do to implement this is: _____

How did things go? What worked well? Why?
_____
_____

Will I use these ideas again in the future? What changes are needed?
_____

Copyright material from Deborah Blaz and Tom Alsop (2023), *Sparking Creativity in the World Language Classroom: Strategies and Ideas to Build Your Students' Language Skills*, Routledge.

CAPSULE 11 – PRAGMATIC APPROACH

GETTING STARTED

1. Pragmatic lessons use active project-based learning strategies and focus on topics relevant to students' lives. Pick a tried-and-true practical idea to use that you know will be a big hit with students.
2. Do an online search about pragmatic teaching ideas for the world-language classroom.
3. How do you plan to do your pragmatic idea? **(BE CURIOUS, IMAGINE, CREATE!)**
4. What materials will you need? Have lots of options for selections of materials.

FOR YOUR CONSIDERATION

1. Think about using pragmatic ideas for learning stations, differentiated instruction and/or multiple intelligences. What ACTFL standard(s) will be addressed with this activity?
2. Will you pick some practical ideas to teach vocabulary, grammar, culture, readers, videos, instruction with apps? Which ones?
3. Will you identify differences and similarities between learners' interests and styles of learning?
4. What student assessment will you use? How will you grade?
5. Will you serve more as teacher-facilitator or as director of most of the learning activities? **(BE FLEXIBLE!)**

TIME TO BRAINSTORM

1. Applaud the active learning going on while students utilize your practical ideas.
2. Speak with colleagues about their favorite practical teaching ideas – ones that work.
3. Invent an easy-to-use grading scale for this teaching strategy.
4. Invite an administrator to watch your class in action.

Copyright material from Deborah Blaz and Tom Alsop (2023), *Sparking Creativity in the World Language Classroom: Strategies and Ideas to Build Your Students' Language Skills*, Routledge.

5. Imagine other creative ideas to include while using your practical ideas in the classroom. Take pictures and/or video of your students working! Share those with the class.

CALL TO ACTION

1. **DO IT!**
2. **CELEBRATE! SHOW YOUR CREATIVITY!**
3. Celebrate your students' successes. Award certificates of creativity to all (see Chapter 10).
4. Award special prizes to the most creative students (stickers, candy, fake money).
5. Celebrate your successes with colleagues at a departmental party. **CELEBRATE POSITIVITY!**
6. Invite a colleague to help you plan your next pragmatic approach extravaganza.
7. **CELEBRATE CREATIVITY!** Who can make the most creative poster about your pragmatic lessons? Decorate the room with the best posters. If using iPads or laptops, make digital posters.
8. Plan a lesson with a colleague who teaches the same level as you and use the pragmatic approach.

The idea(s) on this page that I'd like to try FIRST:

_____

_____

The first thing I need to do to implement this is: _____

How did things go? What worked well? Why?

_____

_____

Will I use these ideas again in the future? What changes are needed?

_____

Copyright material from Deborah Blaz and Tom Alsop (2023), *Sparking Creativity in the World Language Classroom: Strategies and Ideas to Build Your Students' Language Skills,* Routledge.

6

Teaching Ideas
Goal Setting, Innovation, and Implementation Capsules

Introduction

This chapter offers 13 space capsules* with a variety of teaching ideas. Choose new ideas to try out throughout the school year by putting on your creativity and positivity hat for the journey. Try something NEW! Some of the teaching ideas include strategies for grammar, vocabulary, holidays, food, dance, music, painters, writers and more. Toast to your creativity and positivity. RISK-TAKE!!! HAVE FUN!!! SHOW AND SHARE YOUR CREATIVITY/POSITIVITY!!! VARIETY IS THE SPICE OF LIFE!!!

*Please refer to the Detailed Table of Contents to view a list of each of the 13 space capsules!

CAPSULE 1 – VOCABULARY

GETTING STARTED

1. Why should I focus on vocabulary? Should I focus on vocabulary in context?
2. Do an online search about strategies for teaching vocabulary in world language classes.
3. What are your goals? When and how will you teach vocabulary? Will you teach in small groups, individually, learning stations, choice learning, differentiated instruction, multiple intelligences, etc.
4. What do you need to do to prepare? **(BE CURIOUS, IMAGINE, CREATE!)**
5. What results do you expect?
6. How can I accomplish my goals of teaching vocabulary and vocabulary in context? **(BE FLEXIBLE!)**

FOR YOUR CONSIDERATION

1. Some teaching ideas: flashcards, visuals, games, dictionary, online translator, storytelling, bingo, tic-tac-toe, vocabulary diary, writing stories, matching, win-lose-or-draw, scrambled sentences, scrambled words, scavenger hunt, Google Slides, PowerPoint, songs, charades, make-up sentences, listen to songs and identify vocabulary, describe objects, describe actions, Hedbanz game, Password, question-answer game, and speaking activities such as role plays and problem solving. Have a drawing contest where students draw the vocabulary words for the lesson.
2. Ask students what their favorite activities are for learning vocabulary.
3. Gather materials you will need.
4. Video vocabulary activities you do with the students.
5. Discuss how you teach vocabulary with a colleague. Share ideas!

TIME TO BRAINSTORM

1. Include some of your ideas that are not listed above.
2. Did you meet your goals? What were your successes?

Copyright material from Deborah Blaz and Tom Alsop (2023), *Sparking Creativity in the World Language Classroom: Strategies and Ideas to Build Your Students' Language Skills*, Routledge.

3. Speak with your students. Did they enjoy vocabulary activities? Why or why not?
4. Have an assessment tool to evaluate your students' work. Give all students a grade for their work.

CALL TO ACTION

1. **DO IT!**
2. Ask your students to plan a class with three learning activities for vocabulary.
3. Award a prize to students who have excelled while learning vocabulary. Make someone Vocabulary King or Queen. Reward students with stickers, candy, or bookmarks!
4. **CELEBRATE** the work students do to learn vocabulary. Award a Vocabulary Mastery Certificate!
5. Have a **PURE CREATIVITY AWARD** for those students who demonstrated great creativity while learning vocabulary!

The idea(s) on this page that I'd like to try FIRST:

_____

_____

The first thing I need to do to implement this is: _____

How did things go? What worked well? Why?

_____

_____

Will I use these ideas again in the future? What changes are needed?

_____

CAPSULE 2 – GRAMMAR

GETTING STARTED

1. Why teach grammar? How can I present grammar in a more creative and new way?
2. Do an online search about strategies to teach grammar in a world-language class.
3. What are you going to do? **(BE CURIOUS, IMAGINE, CREATE!)**
4. How can you teach grammar in context? Search online to see some ideas. Remember, students should be able to retain grammar and use it in complete sentences.
5. What results do you expect?
6. Do you need to gather materials to do this? **(BE FLEXIBLE!)**

FOR YOUR CONSIDERATION

1. Think about letting students work in teams. Call them grammar teams. Let students prepare and present grammar concepts in context to the class. Award prizes or extra points to the best teams. Let students pick a name for their team. Students are to use the word in the target language (TL) for verbs, nouns, etc., as their team names. Have four or five teams in each class. Keep score and award extra credit points to the team getting the most points before your next written test on grammar.
2. You can be a facilitator and help students/teams having difficulty learning the grammar concepts. Students can use material in their book, e-book, handouts, or other sources.
3. You may want to do use teams throughout the year for creative enrichment.

TIME TO BRAINSTORM

1. Speak with colleagues in your district or others who have taught grammar in context. Use some of their ideas and add your own to the mix.
2. Invite a colleague to watch your class in action as students learn grammar in context.

Copyright material from Deborah Blaz and Tom Alsop (2023), *Sparking Creativity in the World Language Classroom: Strategies and Ideas to Build Your Students' Language Skills*, Routledge.

3. Invite your principal to watch your class in action.
4. Imagine what other techniques you can use to teach grammar in your classroom. **RISK TAKE** and try **NEW AND IMAGINATIVE WAYS TO TEACH GRAMMAR!**

CALL TO ACTION

1. **DO IT!**
2. Have students create some fun games to play in class to learn the grammar!
3. Award special prizes to the most creative students: stickers, candy, buttons, etc.
4. **CELEBRATE** your **SUCCESSES** with your colleagues. Invent a new way to celebrate.
5. Ask your students to make a **FUTURE** lesson plan on how to teach a new grammar point.
6. Invite a colleague to help you plan your next **GRAMMAR EXTRAVAGANZA**.
7. **CELEBRATE CREATIVITY**! Plan a grammar party with the class, or let the class invent and plan the grammar party! Name each student with a part of speech name: noun, adjective, verb, preposition, adverb, etc.

The idea(s) on this page that I'd like to try FIRST:
_____
_____

The first thing I need to do to implement this is: _____

How did things go? What worked well? Why?
_____
_____

Will I use these ideas again in the future? What changes are needed?
_____

Copyright material from Deborah Blaz and Tom Alsop (2023), *Sparking Creativity in the World Language Classroom: Strategies and Ideas to Build Your Students' Language Skills,* Routledge.

CAPSULE 3 – CULTURE/HOLIDAYS

GETTING STARTED

1. Why teach holidays in world language class? Which are the important ones? Why?
2. Do a search and find information on the important holidays in a TL country. Also search for techniques on teaching about holidays in the TL classroom.
3. What holiday do you wish to teach? Why?
4. How will you teach the holiday? **(BE CURIOUS, IMAGINE, CREATE!)**
5. What materials will you need?
6. Review the **ACTFL's Cultural Practices, Products and Perspectives** online.

FOR YOUR CONSIDERATION

1. Focus on the importance of the holiday. Why is it important to the people? How do they celebrate? What traditions and values of the culture can we observe in the celebration of the holiday? **Have a holiday week in your TL class!**
2. Have students work in teams of six to present their work to the class. Have a team present about what, when, and where the people celebrate, another to present on why the people celebrate the holiday, and another on how the people celebrate. Students can make a digital poster or use regular poster board. You might also have each group prepare a TV commercial on why they should celebrate this special holiday. Include important information about the holiday. If possible, have the group present their commercial to the class in the TL.

   > **ACTFL:** Presentational, Intermediate Mid and above; **CEFR:** B1

3. Video all. Show the video to the class at a later date.
4. Accept your role as teacher-facilitator. **(BE FLEXIBLE!)**

TIME TO BRAINSTORM

1. **BE A CHEERLEADER!** Let the students do the work. Applaud the students.
2. Speak with colleagues in your district or others who have some expertise in teaching holidays in the TL classrooms.
3. Invite a native speaker from the community to speak about the holiday you are celebrating.
4. Invite your department head to view the class and the student presentations.
5. Ask the students to comment on the good aspects of the holiday presentations.
6. **IMAGINE** how else you can teach about a holiday in your classroom.

> **ACTFL:** Interpretive, Intermediate Low and above; **CEFR:** B2

CALL TO ACTION

1. **DO IT!**
2. **HAVE FUN!** Celebrate this holiday with **FOOD.**
3. **CELEBRATE** your students' successes. Award a holiday certificate to all.
4. Award special prizes to the most creative students!
5. **TEACH MORE CULTURE THAN GRAMMAR.**
6. Plan your next holiday to teach. **HAVE FUN!**
7. Have an evening presentation of your holiday celebration for parents!

The idea(s) on this page that I'd like to try FIRST:
_____
_____

The first thing I need to do to implement this is: _____

How did things go? What worked well? Why?
_____
_____

Will I use these ideas again in the future? What changes are needed?
_____

CAPSULE 4 – CULTURE/SONGS/MUSIC

GETTING STARTED

1. Why should I teach music/songs to my TL classes? What are the cultural benefits?
2. Do an online search about strategies for teaching music/song in TL classes.
3. What are your goals?
4. What do you need to do to prepare? **(BE CURIOUS, IMAGINE, CREATE!)**
5. What results do you expect?
6. How can I accomplish my goals of conveying culture via music and song? **(BE FLEXIBLE!)**
7. Review the **ACTFL's Cultural Practices, Products and Perspectives** online.

FOR YOUR CONSIDERATION

1. Select a song to teach. Make it a song popular now or in the past in your TL countries.
2. Select a couple of music students/good singers to introduce the song. Have the students lead the class in song. Project the lyrics onto a screen and make sure they are large enough to easily read. Invite a guitar player, a harmonica player, etc., to play background music. If not available, use a good recording of the song. If a famous singer sings the song, go to YouTube. Find a version done by that singer and use it as a model. Project it for the class to see!

> **ACTFL:** Presentational for performers, Interpretive for the others, Novice Mid and above; **CEFR:** A2+

3. Be a facilitator and cheer leader as you walk about the class while the students sing to encourage all to sing. Award a grade for participation!
4. Video all.
5. If you want to get really daring, invite another colleague to critique your presentation.

Copyright material from Deborah Blaz and Tom Alsop (2023), *Sparking Creativity in the World Language Classroom: Strategies and Ideas to Build Your Students' Language Skills,* Routledge.

TIME TO BRAINSTORM

1. Brainstorm with two colleagues how and why they teach music and songs in the TL classes.
2. Speak with the music, choir, or vocal teacher in your school. Get some suggestions.
3. Invite a music teacher to watch you teaching music and song in your classroom.
4. Did you meet your goals? What were your successes?
5. Speak with your students. Did they enjoy the learning experiences? Why or why not?
6. Have an assessment tool to evaluate your students' work. Give all students a grade for their work.

CALL TO ACTION

1. **DO IT!**
2. Teach one new song each month.
3. Award a grade for students as they present in front of the class. Have them work in teams of four as they sing the song.
4. **CELEBRATE CREATIVITY!** Award prizes and/or certificates to the best individual and small group performers.
5. Serenade other world language classes with a song or two!
6. Do a music/song presentation at a parent-teacher organization (PTO) meeting in the TL!

ACTFL: Presentational, Novice Mid and above; **CEFR:** A2

The idea(s) on this page that I'd like to try FIRST:
_____
_____

The first thing I need to do to implement this is: _____

How did things go? What worked well? Why?
_____
_____

Will I use these ideas again in the future? What changes are needed?
_____

Copyright material from Deborah Blaz and Tom Alsop (2023), *Sparking Creativity in the World Language Classroom: Strategies and Ideas to Build Your Students' Language Skills*, Routledge.

CAPSULE 5 – CULTURE/FOODS

GETTING STARTED

1. Why is it important to teach about the importance of food as a product of culture?
2. Do an online search and find information on foods in TL countries.
3. What do you want your students to learn about food? Vocabulary, authentic products, culture?
4. When will you start? **(BE CURIOUS, IMAGINE, CREATE!)**
5. How will you do this? Will you use online materials, recipe cards, cooking-class setting? How many students will there be in each group?
6. Will you be the primary facilitator? Will you have student facilitators?
7. What strategies can you use to keep all in the TL?
8. Have a fun name for each cooking group! **(BE FLEXIBLE!)**

FOR YOUR CONSIDERATION

1. Give a brief written or visual explanation of your goals for this food project. Mention why food is a product of culture. Try to speak mainly in the TL with your students.
2. Have each group choose a food to highlight/prepare. Make sure they use authentic TL recipes.
3. Choose a captain for each group.
4. Encourage students to ask you and each other questions.
5. Will you video the presentation?
6. How will you grade students' work? A global grade for each group? A grade for each student?

> **ACTFL:** Presentational, Intermediate Mid and above; **CEFR:** B1+

TIME TO BRAINSTORM

1. Have a TV cooking show. Each group has a head chef. They can share the recipe, ingredients, and how to do section with the class. Each group can present their show. Have them make

Copyright material from Deborah Blaz and Tom Alsop (2023), *Sparking Creativity in the World Language Classroom: Strategies and Ideas to Build Your Students' Language Skills,* Routledge.

the show funny! Dress the parts. Award a Golden Globe or Oscar to the best TV show. Take a week to prepare and do the show.
2. Invite the parents to visit and see the presentations or present them at a PTO meeting.
3. Prepare the best recipe after school or in a class. Share the great food with the class.
4. Get comments from students. Have them evaluate this project.
5. **Imagine and invent** some super-creative ideas to use with food.

CALL TO ACTION

1. **DO IT!**
2. Celebrate the success of the food presentations! Maybe a night without homework? Maybe a video? Some extra-credit points.
3. Discuss with the class why food is a product of culture. What are some of the practices associated with food in the culture? Why is food so important in the culture?
4. Invite your principal and department head to watch the TV cooking show presentations.

The idea(s) on this page that I'd like to try FIRST:
_____
_____

The first thing I need to do to implement this is: _____

How did things go? What worked well? Why?
_____
_____

Will I use these ideas again in the future? What changes are needed?
_____

Copyright material from Deborah Blaz and Tom Alsop (2023), *Sparking Creativity in the World Language Classroom: Strategies and Ideas to Build Your Students' Language Skills,* Routledge.

CAPSULE 6 – CULTURE/FAMOUS PAINTERS

GETTING STARTED

1. Why should I teach about famous painters in my world language country (countries)? What are the products of culture? What are the practices and perspectives related to famous painters and paintings? Review the **ACTFL's Cultural Practices, Products and Perspectives** online.
2. Do an online search about strategies for teaching about famous painters in TL classes.
3. When will you do this? How much time will you spend on this?
4. What results do you expect? **(BE CURIOUS, IMAGINE, CREATE!)**
5. How can I accomplish my goals? What materials will I need? **(BE FLEXIBLE!)**

FOR YOUR CONSIDERATION

1. Can you use learning stations or differentiated instruction with this project? How?
2. Meet with an art teacher who has extensive practice teaching about famous painters. Share ideas!
3. Pick one famous painter or a variety of famous painters for students to research.
4. Be a facilitator as you walk about the class while your students work. Help them and **ENCOURAGE** them.
5. Video all.
6. Invite an art teacher to do a special presentation on a painter you have chosen.
7. Invite someone from an art museum to speak about your painter(s).

> **ACTFL:** Presentational, Intermediate Mid and above; **CEFR:** A2+

TIME TO BRAINSTORM

1. Share ideas on painters with your world language colleagues on social media. Do an online presentation of your painter with other schools around the country via distance learning!

Copyright material from Deborah Blaz and Tom Alsop (2023), *Sparking Creativity in the World Language Classroom: Strategies and Ideas to Build Your Students' Language Skills,* Routledge.

2. Have a special day such as Pablo Picasso Day. Let the students dress like Pablo Picasso.
3. Have a **DRAW/PAINT OUT**! Let students draw or paint their own version of an abstract painter in the style of Pablo Picasso.
4. Did you meet your goals? What were your successes?
5. Speak with your students. Did they enjoy the the capsule on culture/famous painters? Why or why not?
6. Have an assessment tool to evaluate your students' work. Give all students a grade for their work.

CALL TO ACTION

1. **DO IT!**
2. Award the Pablo Picasso award to the best student work!
3. Let students work in teams and prepare PowerPoint and video clips on their painter.
4. **CELEBRATE** creativity. Announce this art project in your school paper, over the school announcements, and with posters throughout the school.
5. Invite parents to visit the students' presentations on their painter. **PURE CREATIVITY!**
6. **RISK TAKE!** Do a special world language mural in your community that celebrates five or six great painters who represent painters from TL countries. Celebrate with your entire **COMMUNITY**! Let your students work with local artists to create this community mural!

The idea(s) on this page that I'd like to try FIRST:
_____
_____

The first thing I need to do to implement this is: _____

How did things go? What worked well? Why?
_____
_____

Will I use these ideas again in the future? What changes are needed?
_____

Copyright material from Deborah Blaz and Tom Alsop (2023), *Sparking Creativity in the World Language Classroom: Strategies and Ideas to Build Your Students' Language Skills*, Routledge.

CAPSULE 7 – CULTURE/FAMOUS WRITERS

GETTING STARTED

1. What writer(s) are you going to include in **FAMOUS WRITERS** week? Spend two to five days on the writer(s). **CELEBRATE LITERATURE!** Why are the writers a product of culture? What practices are there to celebrate great writers? Perspectives – Why?
2. Do an online search and find information on your **FAMOUS WRITER(S)**. Look for some teaching strategies/ideas for this.
3. What do you want your students to learn? Culture? Improve their reading skills? Have fun?
4. When will you start? **(BE CURIOUS, IMAGINE, CREATE!)**
5. How will you do this? Will you use learning stations, cooperative groups, choice learning?
6. What materials will you use? Digital materials? How many students will be in each group?

FOR YOUR CONSIDERATION

1. How will you prepare? Will you alter your seating arrangement a bit? Will you use old materials or get new materials?
2. Will you speak only in the TL with your students? In certain cases, it may be fine to speak in English.
3. Choose a captain for each group.
4. How will you grade students' work? A global grade for each group? A grade for each student?
5. Prepare an assessment form for your grading.

ACTFL: Presentational, Novice High and above; **CEFR:** A2+

TIME TO BRAINSTORM

1. Use a variety of materials: readers – short novels, short stories, poems. Let the students read and present summaries of what they read to the class. Use PowerPoint, Google Slides, etc.

Copyright material from Deborah Blaz and Tom Alsop (2023), *Sparking Creativity in the World Language Classroom: Strategies and Ideas to Build Your Students' Language Skills*, Routledge.

2. Allow students to write! Award a writing award for the best story in the world language. The award is in honor of the famous writer(s) that the class is studying.

> **ACTFL:** Presentational, Novice High and above; **CEFR:** A2+

3. Speak with a colleague who can share ideas on how to teach about your famous writer(s). Share ideas with him. What works for her/him/them?
4. Invite a local university literature professor to visit and speak about the famous writer(s).

CALL TO ACTION

1. **DO IT!**
2. **CELEBRATE** the success of the students! Maybe a night without homework? Maybe a food party? A video? Offer special prizes like stickers, buttons, or candy.
3. Award prizes to the presenters. Award prizes for the most improved.
4. Name the writing awards in honor of the writer(s) you are celebrating.
5. Award prizes to the best workers in each group. Why not give all a certificate of achievement award for their efforts?
6. Get comments from students. Have them evaluate this culture activity.
7. Have a dress-up day. Dress like the writer. Call it **Bohemian Day**!

The idea(s) on this page that I'd like to try FIRST:

_____
_____

The first thing I need to do to implement this is: _____

How did things go? What worked well? Why?

_____
_____

Will I use these ideas again in the future? What changes are needed?

_____

Copyright material from Deborah Blaz and Tom Alsop (2023), *Sparking Creativity in the World Language Classroom: Strategies and Ideas to Build Your Students' Language Skills,* Routledge.

CAPSULE 8 – CULTURE/SPORTS

GETTING STARTED

1. Why should I teach about sports? Are sports and athletes products of culture? What are some culture practices related to sports and athletes in TL countries? Why do they do this?
2. Do an online search about strategies for teaching about sports/athletes in world language classes.
3. What are your goals? When and how will you do team teaching? Why do team teaching?
4. What do you need to do to prepare? **(BE CURIOUS, IMAGINE, CREATE!)**
5. What results do you expect? How can I accomplish my goals? **(BE FLEXIBLE!)**

FOR YOUR CONSIDERATION

1. Share your ideas about teaching sports/athlete(s) with another colleague. What can you learn?
2. Select a sport and one famous athlete. Emphasize vocabulary, grammar, and culture impacts.
3. What teaching strategies are you going to use? Small groups? Cooperative groups? Choice learning? Differentiated instruction? Will students make a video?
4. Invite a local sports expert or an athlete on one of your school teams to speak about the sport you select. These players should represent a TL country, if possible.
5. Spend a few days or a week on this fun project. Call it **SPORTS WEEK**.

ACTFL: Presentational, Novice High and above; **CEFR:** A2+

TIME TO BRAINSTORM

1. Have students prepare PowerPoint presentations or Google Slides as they teach the class about the sport or athlete. Make posters including the sport, team, and star athlete.

Copyright material from Deborah Blaz and Tom Alsop (2023), *Sparking Creativity in the World Language Classroom: Strategies and Ideas to Build Your Students' Language Skills*, Routledge.

2. Let the class write a TV commercial and teach a bit on the sport and famous athlete in the commercial.

> **ACTFL:** Presentational, Novice High and above; **CEFR:** A2+

3. Select one of the sports such as basketball or tennis. Have a tournament between two classes in the gym or on the tennis courts!
4. Have an assessment tool to evaluate your students' work. Give all students a grade for their work.

CALL TO ACTION

1. **DO IT!**
2. Did you meet your goals? What were your successes?
3. Speak with your students. Did they enjoy the activities? Why or why not?
4. Award certificates and prizes. **CELEBRATE POSITIVITY!**
5. Have a special **WORLD SPORTS DAY.** Students can dress as athletes and/or focus on one famous athlete in the country studied.
6. **CELEBRATE** creativity! Have both classes prepare a special sweet or candy to toast to the success of your first team-teaching world-language classes!
7. Invite the community to visit World Sports Day. Make it an all-world-language department activity!

The idea(s) on this page that I'd like to try FIRST:
_____
_____

The first thing I need to do to implement this is: _____

How did things go? What worked well? Why?
_____
_____

Will I use these ideas again in the future? What changes are needed?
_____

Copyright material from Deborah Blaz and Tom Alsop (2023), *Sparking Creativity in the World Language Classroom: Strategies and Ideas to Build Your Students' Language Skills,* Routledge.

CAPSULE 9 – CULTURE/DANCE

GETTING STARTED

1. Why teach about dance in TL classes? What are some products, practices, and perspectives of the culture that we can observe in dance?
2. Select a TL country: Do an online search about famous dances of Spain, Japan, Mexico, South America, Central America, the Caribbean, France, Germany, Brazil, Italy, or China.
3. Which dance did you pick to teach? Why? How will you do this? What materials do you need? Maybe the salsa, the tango, the bamba? And for French and German?

> **ACTFL:** Presentational, Novice High and above; **CEFR:** A2+

4. Can you make this into a dance class? Let students watch video clips of the dance on YouTube. Let students prepare presentations to the class. **(BE CURIOUS, IMAGINE, CREATE!)**
5. When will you do this? How many days will the dance-focused classes last? Two days, a week?

FOR YOUR CONSIDERATION

1. Maybe small groups only? A little cooperative learning? Group presentations? Maybe role-plays that simulate a dance instructor with students in a dance class? A dance contest with three or four in a group? A world language version of *Dancing with the Stars*?
2. Have a captain for each group.
3. Invite a local dance expert on the dance you selected to be a guest speaker.
4. Accept your role as teacher-facilitator. **(BE FLEXIBLE!)**
5. Set a time limit for students to complete work.

TIME TO BRAINSTORM

1. Speak with colleagues in your district or others who have some expertise in teaching dance in their classrooms.
2. Invite a colleague to watch your class in action as they practice their dance.

Copyright material from Deborah Blaz and Tom Alsop (2023), *Sparking Creativity in the World Language Classroom: Strategies and Ideas to Build Your Students' Language Skills*, Routledge.

3. Invite an administrator to watch your class in action.
4. Plan a *Dancing with the Stars* or live dance sessions. Have an all-school world language dance and combine all world language classes to present dances from TL countries.

> **ACTFL:** Presentational, Novice Mid and above; **CEFR:** A2

CALL TO ACTION

1. **DO IT!**
2. Applaud the **ACTIVE** learning going on now. **APPLAUD** your students. Be a cheerleader!
3. **CELEBRATE** your students' successes. Award certificates/prizes to all!
4. Award special prizes to the most creative students.
5. Celebrate your successes with your colleagues. Publicize your success at school and on social media!
6. **CELEBRATE CREATIVITY!** Create posters (digital or posterboard) and spread them around in school and on social media.

> **ACTFL:** Presentational, Novice Mid and above; **CEFR:** A1

The idea(s) on this page that I'd like to try FIRST:
_____
_____

The first thing I need to do to implement this is: _____

How did things go? What worked well? Why?
_____
_____

Will I use these ideas again in the future? What changes are needed?
_____

Copyright material from Deborah Blaz and Tom Alsop (2023), *Sparking Creativity in the World Language Classroom: Strategies and Ideas to Build Your Students' Language Skills*, Routledge.

CAPSULE 10 – GAMES/APPS

GETTING STARTED

1. Why should I play games in my world language classrooms? What should I play? When? How often?
2. Do an online search about popular games for world language classes.
3. What are your goals? How long should the game(s) last? Do I want to do live in-person games, virtual games, or games on **APPS**?
4. What do you need to do to prepare? **(BE CURIOUS, IMAGINE, CREATE!)**
5. What results do you expect? **(HAVE FUN! BE FLEXIBLE!)**

FOR YOUR CONSIDERATION

1. How often should I play games in class? Should there be prizes? Why?
2. Here are some traditional games to consider: Tic-tac-toe, bingo, matching, scavenger hunt, UNO, Monopoly, hangman, Pictionary, word searches, word scrambles, Scrabble, charades, guess the celebrity, Boggle, Hedbanz, Taboo, and Scattergories.
3. Here are some digital **APPS** to consider: Duolingo, Lango, Yabla, Kahoot, and Mind Snacks.
4. What teaching strategies are you going to use? Small groups/teams, individual learning. Video all.
5. Spend a few days or a week using games. Use the games to supplement targeted lessons such as vocabulary, grammar, and culture. Call it **GAME WEEK IN WORLD LANGUAGE CLASS!**

TIME TO BRAINSTORM

1. Speak with a world language colleague about her/his opinions of useful games for your world language class.
2. Who will be the host to lead the games? One student or a pair of students.
3. Be sure to review rules of the game and how to play with the class.
4. Tell the students what the prizes will be.

Copyright material from Deborah Blaz and Tom Alsop (2023), *Sparking Creativity in the World Language Classroom: Strategies and Ideas to Build Your Students' Language Skills*, Routledge.

5. Invite a teaching colleague and/or administrator to watch the game day competition.
6. Did you meet your goals? What were your successes?
7. Speak with your students. Did they enjoy the activities? Why or why not?

CALL TO ACTION

1. **DO IT!**
2. Award certificates and prizes. **CELEBRATE POSITIVITY!**
3. Award student participation in the games with some special world language culinary delights.
4. **CELEBRATE** creativity! Toast to the winners of the games with a glass of flavored water!
5. Share video of the students playing the games online on social media! Put pics on the school world language blog/website and the school website. Be sure to get parental approval.

The idea(s) on this page that I'd like to try FIRST:

_____

_____

The first thing I need to do to implement this is: _____

How did things go? What worked well? Why?

_____

_____

Will I use these ideas again in the future? What changes are needed?

_____

CAPSULE 11 – SKITS/THEATER

GETTING STARTED

1. What value do skits have in learning a world language? Do skits provide ways for students to orally communicate and socialize in the TL?
2. Select a skit for students to practice and perform in class. How will you grade the students' work?
3. Provide time for students to prepare the skit. It could be a short fun skit, a shortened form of a fairy tale, or a scene from an easy-to-follow play. Let your students write a short play in the TL.
4. Use everyday pieces of life to use as skits: problems at home, car trouble, at a party, at a dance, a funny episode in Spanish class, etc. **(BE CURIOUS, IMAGINE, CREATE!)**
5. When will you do this? How long will the skits be in the world language?

FOR YOUR CONSIDERATION

1. Will you use groups of three or four or work in pairs? How will you grade the skits? Use an easy-to-use grading scale: 5 – outstanding, 4 – good, 3 – average, 2 – so-so, 1 – needs work, very weak.
2. Have students dress up for their skit, bring props, and include music in the background.

> **ACTFL:** Presentational, Novice High and above; **CEFR:** A2

3. Have students use short stories to act out. Act out a chapter from a short novel.
4. Have one student in each group be the director. Video each presentation!
5. Accept your role as teacher-facilitator. **(BE FLEXIBLE!)**
6. Set a time limit for students to complete work.

TIME TO BRAINSTORM

1. Speak with your colleagues and share ideas about how to prepare and teach skits for world language class.

Copyright material from Deborah Blaz and Tom Alsop (2023), *Sparking Creativity in the World Language Classroom: Strategies and Ideas to Build Your Students' Language Skills*, Routledge.

2. Speak with a theater, drama teacher in your school. Get some acting tips from her/him/them.
3. Invite a guest speaker/actor/actress to speak to the class about acting.
4. Invite the head of your department to watch your class in action as they perform their skits.
5. Have a skit competition. Appoint two students to be judges.
6. Perform your skits at a PTO meeting or at a World Language Dinner Theater.

CALL TO ACTION

1. **DO IT!**
2. **CELEBRATE** your students' successes! Award a **Golden Globe** or **Oscar** to the best actors/actresses!
3. Award special prizes to the best group performance.
4. Publicize the winning actors/actresses on social media, the school newspaper, and school website. Be sure to get parental approval.
5. Have special awards for the best costumes, musical background, or song and best director!
6. **CELEBRATE CREATIVITY!** Take photos of each group of actors and use as digital posters!

The idea(s) on this page that I'd like to try FIRST:

_____

_____

The first thing I need to do to implement this is: _____

How did things go? What worked well? Why?

_____

_____

Will I use these ideas again in the future? What changes are needed?

_____

Copyright material from Deborah Blaz and Tom Alsop (2023), *Sparking Creativity in the World Language Classroom: Strategies and Ideas to Build Your Students' Language Skills,* Routledge.

CAPSULE 12 – PUPPET SHOWS

GETTING STARTED

1. Why have students make puppets? How will using puppets help students?
2. Do an Internet search for information about ideas for using puppet shows in the world language class.
3. Will your students make paper bag puppets, sock puppets, cardboard puppets, or finger puppets?
4. What will the students do with the puppets? **(BE CURIOUS, IMAGINE, CREATE!)**
5. When will you do this? How many days will the puppet show run? How will you grade this?
6. Will students make a small puppet theater for use in your world language class? Have a student make you a puppet theater in her/his shop class. Or find a parent skilled in carpentry to make you a small puppet theater to use in your world language class.
7. How will this be graded? Consider having students help make the rubric.

FOR YOUR CONSIDERATION

1. Have students work in pairs or in groups of three. Have a captain for each group. Assign roles.
2. Have students include a cultural theme with the puppets! Maybe a famous writer, painter, inventor, athlete, singer, etc. The puppets could be animals, fruits, or food native to the country.
3. Pay attention to learners' interests and styles of learning.
4. Accept your role as teacher-facilitator. **(BE FLEXIBLE!)**
5. Set a time limit, perhaps one class to make puppets, another class to prepare the dialogue/script, and one more class to present at the puppet theater in front of the class. If you have no real theater, have students kneel behind the teacher's desk.

Copyright material from Deborah Blaz and Tom Alsop (2023), *Sparking Creativity in the World Language Classroom: Strategies and Ideas to Build Your Students' Language Skills,* Routledge.

TIME TO BRAINSTORM

1. Applaud the **ACTIVE** learning going on now. **APPLAUD** your students. Be a cheerleader!
2. Speak with local puppeteers in your community and ask them for their ideas.
3. Invite a local puppeteer to visit your class to speak about the creative expression that occurs while making and using puppets.
4. Invite your principal or assistant principal to watch your class in action.
5. Make posters in the TL to promote the upcoming puppet shows.
6. Video the puppet presentations. Present your puppet show to the entire school.
7. Have a **World Language Department Puppet Show** in front of the entire student body.

> **ACTFL:** Presentational, Novice High and above; **CEFR:** B1

CALL TO ACTION

1. **DO IT!**
2. **CELEBRATE!** Award the best puppet creator and actor/actress awards to outstanding students, most unique puppet, etc.
3. Publicize your success at school and on social media. Use your school or world language website.
4. Publicize the success of your puppet shows in the local newspapers and on digital media. Invite a TV station to come and watch the performances!

The idea(s) on this page that I'd like to try FIRST:
_____
_____

The first thing I need to do to implement this is: _____

How did things go? What worked well? Why?
_____
_____

Will I use these ideas again in the future? What changes are needed?
_____

Copyright material from Deborah Blaz and Tom Alsop (2023), *Sparking Creativity in the World Language Classroom: Strategies and Ideas to Build Your Students' Language Skills,* Routledge.

CAPSULE 13 – COMMERCIALS

GETTING STARTED

1. Why is it a good idea to let students invent and act in TV commercials in the TL?
2. Do an online search to discover how you might use TV commercials in the TL class. Find some TL TV commercials of familiar products.
3. What popular TV commercials do you want your students to do in the TL?
4. How can students create their own products/TV commercials? **(BE CURIOUS, IMAGINE, CREATE!)**
5. What materials will they need?
6. Call this special day **Zany TV Commercials Day.**

FOR YOUR CONSIDERATION

1. Focus on the importance of the commercials. Why are they important to the people?

> **ACTFL:** Presentational, Intermediate Low and above; **CEFR:** B1

2. Have students work in groups of four to present their version of a TV commercial. The version can be a foreign product or one that is well-known in the United States.
3. Have each group present their TV commercial in the TL. Students should bring props and dress the part.
4. Video all TV commercials. Show the video to the class at a later date.
5. Accept your role as teacher-facilitator. **(BE FLEXIBLE!)**

TIME TO BRAINSTORM

1. **BE A CHEERLEADER. LET THE STUDENTS DO THE WORK. APPLAUD THE STUDENTS!**
2. Speak with colleagues in your district or others who have experience in doing TV commercials with their classes.
3. Invite your department head to view the class and the student presentations.

4. Ask the students to comment on the fun things they learned while doing TV commercials.
5. **IMAGINE** how else you can teach TV commercials in class. Have students make and act-out some zany TV commercials for such new products as a special toothpaste, a super-healthy new diet drink, a new special toilet paper, a new and special shampoo or soap, a new and special electric car, a new and special TV, and a new and special book to use to learn the TL.

> **ACTFL:** Presentational, Novice High and above; **CEFR:** A2+

CALL TO ACTION

1. **DO IT. HAVE FUN!**
2. CELEBRATE your students' successes. Award a **Creative TV Commercials Award!**
3. Award special prizes to the most creative students.
4. **SPEAK MORE in the TL and have fun with the TV commercials!**
5. Let the students present their TV commercials at a PTO meeting. Post some of their fun videos onto YouTube!

The idea(s) on this page that I'd like to try FIRST:

_____

_____

The first thing I need to do to implement this is: _____

How did things go? What worked well? Why?

_____

_____

Will I use these ideas again in the future? What changes are needed?

_____

Copyright material from Deborah Blaz and Tom Alsop (2023), *Sparking Creativity in the World Language Classroom: Strategies and Ideas to Build Your Students' Language Skills*, Routledge.

7

Promotional Ideas
Goal Setting, Innovation, and Implementation Capsules

Introduction

This chapter provides nine space capsules* that help promote world languages. Choose different ideas to try out as the school year progresses. Put on your creativity and positivity hat for the journey. Toast to your creativity and positivity! Some of the promotional ideas include a talent show, podcast or radio show, market day, world language clubs, and more! TAKE RISKS!!! HAVE FUN!!! SHOW AND SHARE YOUR CREATIVITY/POSITIVITY!!! VARIETY IS THE SPICE OF LIFE!

*Please refer to the Detailed Table of Contents to view a list of each of the nine promotional ideas space capsules!

CAPSULE 1 – TALENT SHOW

GETTING STARTED

1. How can I plan a **talent show?** Why do this? What are the benefits?
2. Do an online search for information about world language talent shows.
3. What are your goals? When and how will you do the talent shows? Will all world languages be represented in the talent show?
4. What do you need to do to prepare? **(BE CURIOUS, IMAGINE, CREATE!)**
5. What results do you expect? Will you invite parents, other relatives, administrators, etc.?
6. How can I accomplish my language and culture learning targets via a talent show? **(BE FLEXIBLE!)**

FOR YOUR CONSIDERATION

1. What are your categories? Song, dance, speeches, comedy – joke telling, skits – plays, poetry readings, musical instruments – guitar, etc., with world language music?

> **ACTFL:** Presentational, Intermediate Mid and above; **CEFR:** B1+

2. Select a student host from each language to present the acts in each world language. Make sure all presentations are in the world language.
3. Be a facilitator and cheer leader as you walk about the class while the students prepare for the show. Encourage all to be in the talent show. Award a grade for participation.
4. Video all.
5. Practice several times before the event. You may wish to practice before or after school.

TIME TO BRAINSTORM

1. Brainstorm with a music teacher and a drama/theater teacher. Listen to their suggestions on how to stage a talent show. What props will you need? How many people do you invite?

Copyright material from Deborah Blaz and Tom Alsop (2023), *Sparking Creativity in the World Language Classroom: Strategies and Ideas to Build Your Students' Language Skills*, Routledge.

2. Where will the show take place? Will you charge admission? Use the money from ticket sales to buy materials for the world language department and for travel/study scholarships.
3. Invite members of the community to judge the events. Try to have native speakers as judges.
4. Have the hosts say a few words about the importance of world language study.
5. Did you meet your goals? What were your successes?
6. Speak with your students. Did they enjoy the learning experiences? Why or why not?

CALL TO ACTION

1. **DO IT!**
2. **CELEBRATE** creativity! Award prizes and/or certificates to the best individual and small group performers. Have Golden Oscar, Silver Tony, Bronze Emmy, or Golden Globe awards.
3. Publicize the event before and after. **ENCOURAGE** the community to attend – anyone interested in supporting world language study! Publicize on websites, social media, YouTube, community newspapers, flyers, etc.
4. Invite TV stations to attend and help promote the event before and after.
5. Invite all administrators in your school, the school superintendent and school board to attend!
6. Take video of the entire show and interview the guests on your version of the red carpet!

The idea(s) on this page that I'd like to try FIRST:
_____

The first thing I need to do to implement this is: _____

How did things go? What worked well? Why?
_____

Will I use these ideas again in the future? What changes are needed?
_____

Copyright material from Deborah Blaz and Tom Alsop (2023), *Sparking Creativity in the World Language Classroom: Strategies and Ideas to Build Your Students' Language Skills,* Routledge.

CAPSULE 2 – PODCAST/RADIO SHOW

GETTING STARTED

1. Why do I want to have a **podcast/radio show**? Can I involve the community? Do I want to do the show in English or in my world language?
2. Do an online search on how to set-up a world language podcast.
3. How long will my podcast last? What will I call the podcast?
4. Why do I want to do a podcast? Will it be on once a month, every two months? Will the students host the show, or will I be the host?
5. What will I talk about? **(BE CURIOUS, IMAGINE, CREATE!)**
6. What materials do I need?

FOR YOUR CONSIDERATION

1. Use a quality desktop or a laptop with a good microphone. Consider creating a Zoom account to record the show on your laptop or desktop. You could also use FaceTime on an Apple device and record only the audio.
2. Have your students, parents, and community members be guests on your podcast.
3. Use a microphone to record. Save the audio recording onto a storage site such as SoundCloud. From SoundCloud, link the show to the podcast site. See Chapter 8 for more sites to use.
4. Use a song intro to open and close each show.

TIME TO BRAINSTORM

1. Select topics such as culture, grammar, speaking practices, vocabulary, writing, and listening. Promote the TL. Why is important for all to study and learn a world language and its culture?
2. Speak with colleagues in your district or others who have made a podcast. What are some potential problems to be aware of?
3. Invite a colleague or student to be on your podcast. Let them pick a world language topic they wish to discuss.

Copyright material from Deborah Blaz and Tom Alsop (2023), *Sparking Creativity in the World Language Classroom: Strategies and Ideas to Build Your Students' Language Skills,* Routledge.

4. Invite an administrator to be on your podcast. Speak about the importance of studying a world language.
5. You can also do a podcast with other world language teachers and native speakers in world language countries by using Skype or Zoom. Simply record the audio portion. You then turn that into an Mp3 file, download, and then put the audio file onto your podcast storage provider and Apple Podcast Connect.

CALL TO ACTION

1. **DO IT!**
2. **CELEBRATE** your show! Announce it over social media so others can hear the show. Encourage them to follow your show by signing on to receive all shows via their e-mails.
3. Assign a show for your students as an assignment. They are to listen to your podcast and write a review of what you discuss. The review should include details of what was said.
4. Invite a guest who has appeared on your show to speak at school about the importance of world language study.

The idea(s) on this page that I'd like to try FIRST:

_____
_____

The first thing I need to do to implement this is: _____

How did things go? What worked well? Why?

_____
_____

Will I use these ideas again in the future? What changes are needed?

_____

Copyright material from Deborah Blaz and Tom Alsop (2023), *Sparking Creativity in the World Language Classroom: Strategies and Ideas to Build Your Students' Language Skills,* Routledge.

CAPSULE 3 – MARKET DAY

GETTING STARTED

1. Why have a **market day?** What are some products, practices, and perspectives of the culture that can be observed at this language market day? Do an online search.
2. What products could your world language students sell at your booth that reflect TL culture?
3. Will students speak only in the TL? Will all language teachers and students participate?
4. Will you sell fruits, vegetables, candies, pastries? **(BE CURIOUS, IMAGINE, CREATE!)**
5. Who will make and bring the food? Will you purchase some of the food at local world language groceries?

FOR YOUR CONSIDERATION

1. Set a date. Will you have this event in the evening? During the week? On a weekend?
2. Where will you have the event? In the school gym? A neighboring shopping mall? A farmers' market?
3. Will you invite all the community? How will you publicize the event?
4. Will you charge for the food? Can you use profits from the sales to buy materials for your world language department or can you send the money to a world language country to help improve the lives of others?
5. Let the students organize the event. Set a time limit for students to complete work.
6. Accept your role as teacher-facilitator. **(BE FLEXIBLE!)**

TIME TO BRAINSTORM

1. Applaud the **ACTIVE** learning going on now. **APPLAUD** your students. Be a **CHEERLEADER!**
2. Speak with colleagues in your district or others who have some expertise in doing community market days.

Copyright material from Deborah Blaz and Tom Alsop (2023), *Sparking Creativity in the World Language Classroom: Strategies and Ideas to Build Your Students' Language Skills*, Routledge.

3. Invite colleagues, administrators, parents, and the entire community to this special event.
4. Let students create foreign currency – make-believe – to use to purchase the foods at the stands. Shoppers can change dollars and receive the make-believe currency of the TL country.
5. Have students dress with native-like dress.
6. Play music in the TL in the background while shoppers pass through the market.
7. Have students make signs for their market stands in the target language. Search online for examples.

ACTFL: Culture: Practices and Presentational, Novice Mid and above; **CEFR:** A1

8. Video the event and share the video on social media.
9. Invite the mayor of the city. Invite the governor.
10. Have students be roving minstrels as they stroll around the booths serenading visitors with songs in the TL.

ACTFL: Presentational, Intermediate Low; **CEFR:** A2

CALL TO ACTION

1. **DO IT!** Do the celebration during a special class. Invite other classes?
2. **CELEBRATE** your students' successes! Award certificates or prizes to all who help organize and work at the market.
3. Decorate your room with photos from the event or do a bulletin board in the hallway.

The idea(s) on this page that I'd like to try FIRST:
_____

The first thing I need to do to implement this is: _____

How did things go? What worked well? Why?
_____

Will I use these ideas again in the future? What changes are needed?
_____

CAPSULE 4 – DINNER THEATER

GETTING STARTED

1. Why have a **dinner theater**? What are some products, practices, and perspectives of the culture that we can observe during the dinner theater?
2. When do you want to do a dinner theater? What students will participate? What will you do at the theater? Which world languages will participate? One, two, all of them?
3. What materials will you need? Where will you have the **dinner theater**?
4. How long will the dinner theater last? **(BE CURIOUS, IMAGINE, CREATE!)**

FOR YOUR CONSIDERATION

1. Will your students perform a play in the TL?
2. Will your students sing some songs in the TL?
3. Will your students be wait staff and take orders in the TL?
4. Will your language students make the meal? Will it be international cuisine? **(BE FLEXIBLE!)**
5. Which students will lead organize and lead the dinner theater team as they plan the event?

TIME TO BRAINSTORM

1. Applaud the **ACTIVE** learning going on now. **APPLAUD** your students. Be a cheerleader!
2. Speak with colleagues in other schools who have tried dinner theaters.
3. Search online to see if there have been similar events done around the country.
4. Have students only speak the TL during the dinner theater.

> **ACTFL:** Interpersonal, Intermediate Mid and above; **CEFR:** B1+

Copyright material from Deborah Blaz and Tom Alsop (2023), *Sparking Creativity in the World Language Classroom: Strategies and Ideas to Build Your Students' Language Skills,* Routledge.

5. Pick a fun play for the students to act out. Pick a play that students can do without a super effort.

ACTFL: Presentational, Intermediate Mid and above; **CEFR:** B1+

6. Select some poems in the world language for the students to recite in a dramatic reading of the poem.

ACTFL: Presentational, Novice High and above; **CEFR:** A2

7. Ask parents and the community to assist you with this project. They could be great sources to help promote the event. Use social media!
8. Sell tickets to the event. Use any profits to purchase educational materials for the world language classroom or offer a small scholarship to a deserving world language student.
9. Allow students to make posters to promote the event.

CALL TO ACTION

1. **DO IT!** List the benefits to your students and the department before doing this.
2. Publicize your success at school and on social media!
3. **CELEBRATE CREATIVITY!** Create posters – digital or other – and spread them around in school and on social media!
4. Take pictures of the event.
5. Video the event!
6. Invite local TV stations to attend and promote the event!
7. Invite a well-known political figure to the event!
8. Invite a well-known athlete to the event!

The idea(s) on this page that I'd like to try FIRST:
_____

The first thing I need to do to implement this is: _____

How did things go? What worked well? Why?
_____

Will I use these ideas again in the future? What changes are needed?
_____

Copyright material from Deborah Blaz and Tom Alsop (2023), *Sparking Creativity in the World Language Classroom: Strategies and Ideas to Build Your Students' Language Skills,* Routledge.

CAPSULE 5 – LANGUAGE CARNIVAL

GETTING STARTED

1. Why do you want to have a **carnival**? Will the entire world language department participate?
2. Do an online search and find some schools who have done a language carnival.
3. What booths will you have at this carnival?
4. What students will help organize the event? **(BE CURIOUS, IMAGINE, CREATE!)**
5. When will you do this? How many days will the carnival last?
6. Where will the world language carnival take place?
7. Will there be tickets to purchase to play the games at the booths?
8. How will the world language department use the funds made from this event?

FOR YOUR CONSIDERATION

1. What activities/games will you have at each booth?
2. Consider having grammar, vocabulary, alphabet, and culture games at each booth.
3. Have world language apps games at a booth or two.
4. What students will help you organize the event? **(BE FLEXIBLE!)**
5. Set a date. Have the event for two days. Students are to listen and speak in the TL while playing the games.

> **ACTFL:** Interpersonal, Novice High; **CEFR:** B1

6. Have prizes at each booth.
7. Have games for individual participation and others for groups of two or three students.

TIME TO BRAINSTORM

1. Let's think of some fun games: vocabulary/grammar hangman, missing-letter, missing-words, guess someone's weight or age in the world language, grammar/vocabulary categories, culture/sports/soccer stars or teams, soccer kicking contests, basketball games

like 2-on-2 (speak only in the world language) or free-throw shooting (say numbers in the TL for each free-throw made), drawing contest (draw sentences in the TL), word/vocabulary charades, karaoke (sing along song in the TL), poetry reading booth, or a world-language dance booth (award prizes for students who try to learn a few steps to a world language dance). Award prizes at each booth. Make all signs for booths in the TL.

2. Have speaking booths. Students who play speak in a TL. Give prizes when students say five sentences in the TL. Have another game where students describe objects in the TL. Have an "Answer the Question in a TL" game.

ACTFL: Interpersonal, Intermediate Low; **CEFR:** B1+

3. Invite school administrators to the event.
4. Applaud the **ACTIVE** learning going on now. **APPLAUD** your students. **BE A CHEERLEADER!**

CALL TO ACTION

1. **DO IT!** Invite TV stations to this special day!
2. Video this special event. Take lots of pics!
3. **CELEBRATE** your students' successes! Award certificates/prizes to all!
4. Celebrate your successes with your colleagues. Publicize your success at school and on social media!

The idea(s) on this page that I'd like to try FIRST:

_____

_____

The first thing I need to do to implement this is: _____

How did things go? What worked well? Why?

_____

_____

Will I use these ideas again in the future? What changes are needed?

_____

Copyright material from Deborah Blaz and Tom Alsop (2023), *Sparking Creativity in the World Language Classroom: Strategies and Ideas to Build Your Students' Language Skills,* Routledge.

CAPSULE 6 – TEACHER/STUDENT/PARENT TRAVEL

GETTING STARTED

1. Why do student travel? How does student travel enhance world-language learning?
2. Do an online search and look for student travel companies. Which programs are the better ones?
3. You can travel with your students. Many companies offer a free trip to teachers if they have a certain number of participants.
4. Speak with your students. Are they interested in student travel? Why or why not?
5. When will you do this? Over spring break? In the summer? On a fall recess?

FOR YOUR CONSIDERATION

1. How will you promote student travel? Show video clips of student travel in the city (cities) you select to visit.
2. Do you have any ideas to help students raise money to help them with the cost? Will community businesses donate?
3. Allow parents to travel with your group. They can count toward the maximum number of participants so you can then get a free trip!
4. Parents can also help chaperone. **(BE FLEXIBLE!)**
5. Set a time/meeting with students who are interested in the trip. Invite someone from the travel company to come to the meeting and give details about the trip.
6. Get administrative approval before you meet with the students/parents.
7. Make creative posters announcing the trip. Share the promo on social media and in the community!

TIME TO BRAINSTORM

1. APPLAUD STUDENT INTEREST on going on the trip!
2. Chat with colleagues who have traveled out of the country with student groups.

Copyright material from Deborah Blaz and Tom Alsop (2023), *Sparking Creativity in the World Language Classroom: Strategies and Ideas to Build Your Students' Language Skills,* Routledge.

3. Have a student speak to the class that has already experienced overseas travel.
4. Have students sign a permission form that releases you and your school district from any lawsuits stemming from trip incidents. Have students start a travel diary that details daily preparation for the upcoming trip and then details of daily activities while in the country.
5. Focus on the culture pertinent to the country(ies) you will be visiting. Teach and discuss culture highlights with your students.
6. Have a final meeting with parents and students. Review a packing list and discuss evening curfews for students while they are traveling. Present and discuss the currency of the country you are visiting. Publicize and celebrate those who are traveling.

CALL TO ACTION

1. **DO IT!**
2. **CELEBRATE** your students' decision to travel. Have them bring cultural realia to class upon their return. Let the students speak about their experiences and discuss why they loved the trip!
3. Publicize the return of the students. Let the students post their photos, videos, and realia on social media. Publicize their experiences in the school newspaper and website!

The idea(s) on this page that I'd like to try FIRST:

_____
_____

The first thing I need to do to implement this is: _____

How did things go? What worked well? Why?

_____
_____

Will I use these ideas again in the future? What changes are needed?

_____

Copyright material from Deborah Blaz and Tom Alsop (2023), *Sparking Creativity in the World Language Classroom: Strategies and Ideas to Build Your Students' Language Skills*, Routledge.

CAPSULE 7 – PRIZES/AWARDS

GETTING STARTED

1. Why should I have awards/prizes for students? What are some prizes that I could give for outstanding student achievement and participation?
2. When should I give these awards? How can I do this (see Chapter 10.)?
3. How often can I give these awards? **(BE CURIOUS, IMAGINE, CREATE!)**
4. What role does competition have in education? Should we award effort and achievement? What benefits will come from giving awards?

FOR YOUR CONSIDERATION

1. Award prizes to individuals and small groups, as many as possible (see Chapter 10).
2. Here are some possible prizes: stickers, buttons, achievement certificates, or ribbons. You may also award coupons. You can make these quickly. Have coupons such as No Homework Coupons, Extra-Credit Points Coupons for written and/or oral tests. **(BE FLEXIBLE!)**
3. Have awards for the student(s) of the week, of the month, or of the semester!
4. Have a Best Participation in Class award, a Group of the Week award, the **Vocabulary Star of the Week**, the **Grammar Star of the Week**, and the **Best Speaker Award** - Individual and/or Group. Ask students to dream up some categories!
5. Have **World Language Golden Oscar Awards** for various world-language skills such as listening, speaking, reading, writing: best speakers, best readers, best writers, best skits, etc.

TIME TO BRAINSTORM

1. Applaud the **ACTIVE** learning going on that the awards help create. **APPLAUD** your students. Be a **CHEERLEADER!**
2. Speak with colleagues at your school or online to share ideas on prizes and awards.

3. Video your top achievers for their effort each week and share with parents.
4. Take pictures of your top achievers. Recognize them by putting the photos onto the bulletin board (or your website).
5. Announce the top students in your world language classes in the daily school announcements, on the radio, posters around the school, and social media. **CELEBRATE SUCCESS!**
6. Have a **World Language Honor Roll.** Recognize the top five world language students in each language at the end of each grading period!
7. Keep a scoreboard on your bulletin board with individual students' names and group/team names as students compete throughout the semester!

CALL TO ACTION

1. **DO IT! CELEBRATE** all the efforts and achievements of you and your students and **STAY ENERGIZED!**
2. Award **SPECIAL PRIZES FOR STUDENT CREATIVITY!**
3. Have a world language party in honor of your award-winning students!

The idea(s) on this page that I'd like to try FIRST:

_____

_____

The first thing I need to do to implement this is: _____

How did things go? What worked well? Why?

_____

_____

Will I use these ideas again in the future? What changes are needed?

_____

CAPSULE 8 – PROFESSIONAL DEVELOPMENT

GETTING STARTED: Remember, professional development translates into *better teaching*!

1. Why should I continue my professional development? What aspects of teaching do I want to improve? What positive things will happen when I take advantage of professional development opportunities?
2. Do an online search about professional development for world-language teachers.
3. What do you need to do to take advantage of professional development opportunities (permission, funding, etc.)? **(BE CURIOUS, IMAGINE, CREATE!)**
4. When will you participate in some professional development? **(BE FLEXIBLE!)**

FOR YOUR CONSIDERATION

1. Professional world language organizations such as ACTFL, AATs for all languages, NECTFL, CSCTFL, SWCOLT and the PNCFL are some popular national and regional organizations that have outstanding conferences and informative websites as well as social media groups on various platforms such as Facebook, etc.
2. Statewide language groups also are quite good and often have exciting professional opportunities.
3. There are also summer teacher programs and scholarships for world language teachers to study language, methodologies, and improve their language skills. Check those out online.
4. Participate in any teacher in-service in your school district.
5. Be a presenter at world language conferences!
6. Offer your services to world language organizations and serve as an officer, etc.
7. Write a book or supplemental materials for use in world language classes. Get your work published!
8. Create an app for world language classes!

Copyright material from Deborah Blaz and Tom Alsop (2023), *Sparking Creativity in the World Language Classroom: Strategies and Ideas to Build Your Students' Language Skills,* Routledge.

TIME TO BRAINSTORM

1. Include some of your ideas that are not listed above.
2. Speak with a colleague and share ideas on professional development.
3. Who is your favorite leader in world language organizations? Why? **CAN YOU BE THAT LEADER?**

CALL TO ACTION

1. **DO IT!** Your target is to participate in a world language organization as a presenter, volunteer, or officer!
2. **CELEBRATE YOUR PROFESSIONAL DEVELOPMENT** with your principal and department head! Did you meet your goals? What were your successes?

The idea(s) on this page that I'd like to try FIRST:
_____
_____

The first thing I need to do to implement this is: _____

How did things go? What worked well? Why?
_____
_____

Will I use these ideas again in the future? What changes are needed?
_____

Copyright material from Deborah Blaz and Tom Alsop (2023), *Sparking Creativity in the World Language Classroom: Strategies and Ideas to Build Your Students' Language Skills,* Routledge.

CAPSULE 9 – LANGUAGE CLUBS

GETTING STARTED

1. Why have a language club? How will you organize the club? Will it include all world languages in your department or your language only?
2. Do an online search about strategies to help organize the organization of your TL club. Who will help you organize the club?
3. When will you have your club? How long will each meeting last? **(BE FLEXIBLE!)**
4. Give the club a name (famous author, painter, singer, etc.).
5. What activities do you want to include for the club? **(BE CURIOUS, IMAGINE, CREATE!)**
6. What results do you expect?

FOR YOUR CONSIDERATION

1. Have students sign up for the club. Elect officers. Allow the officers to organize and plan each club. Let the students do most of the work.
2. You should be a facilitator. Allow students to make decisions on what to do, when to do it, gather materials for each meeting, and say why they want to do the activity.
3. Have a world language club initiation. Have a **Mission Statement** for the students to read as their oath to the club. Have a candlelight ceremony. Invite parents. Award students **Certificates of Initiation**!
4. Have some fundraising events to raise money for your world-language department!

TIME TO BRAINSTORM

1. Speak with colleagues in other school districts to share their ideas on how to start a world language club.
2. Celebrate TL holidays with your club!
3. Invite your principal to watch your TL club in action!
4. Let the TL club organize and sponsor these type of events: Have a TL dance lesson, sing TL songs, have a world language dance, a TL

puppet show, a TL choir, a TL cooking contest, a world language softball game, a world language soccer game, a world language basketball game, a TL poetry jam, a TL storytelling contest, plan a trip to a TL country, a TL radio/TV show, a world language tennis match, a trip to an art museum to see famous paintings done by international masters, and birthday parties to celebrate the birthdays of TL club members! **RISK TAKE** and try **NEW AND IMAGINATIVE IDEAS** in your world language club!

CALL TO ACTION

1. **DO IT!**
2. **CELEBRATE** your TL club **SUCCESSES** with your students! Create a new way to celebrate!
3. Ask your students to video each TL club meeting. Share your video with other schools to encourage them to have their own TL club!
4. **CELEBRATE CREATIVITY**! Award special TL club pins to the club members. Award the officers of the club a copy of a famous world language painting. Make it an affordable/inexpensive copy.
5. **PUBLICIZE** all TL events/activities on your school website and on social media!

CAPSULE NAME/TOPIC_____

GETTING STARTED

1. _____
2. _____
3. _____
4. _____
5. _____

FOR YOUR CONSIDERATION

1. _____
2. _____
3. _____
4. _____
5. _____

TIME TO BRAINSTORM

1. _____
2. _____
3. _____
4. _____
5. _____

CALL TO ACTION

1. _____
2. _____
3. _____
4. _____

Copyright material from Deborah Blaz and Tom Alsop (2023), *Sparking Creativity in the World Language Classroom: Strategies and Ideas to Build Your Students' Language Skills,* Routledge.

The idea(s) on this page that I'd like to try FIRST:
_____
_____

The first thing I need to do to implement this is: _____

How did things go? What worked well? Why?
_____
_____

Will I use these ideas again in the future? What changes are needed?
_____

Copyright material from Deborah Blaz and Tom Alsop (2023), *Sparking Creativity in the World Language Classroom: Strategies and Ideas to Build Your Students' Language Skills,* Routledge.

8

Support
Making the Creative Journey Fun and Easy

Introduction

This chapter provides **sources of support** to make the **creative journey fun and easy**. There are two levels of support, human support and technology support. Included in the human support are six sources of support: our teacher colleagues, our students, parents, administrators, those living and working in the community and also our own unique supporter, ourselves. We need to toot our own horn.

The seventh source of support is technology support, including computer apps, world language software, games, social media and other useful technology sources that can be found online.

These levels of support make our creative journey more fun and easy. There is strength in numbers.

There are two **Planner Support Pages**, one for the human support sources and one for the technology support sources. These pages allow us, as well as our sources of support, to plan and evaluate how things went on the creative journey. You can find one of these at the end of the human support sources section (6-Myself) and the other at the end of the technology sources.

Human Sources of Support 1 – Teacher Colleagues

One important expression I want to emphasize is this one: **TAKE RISKS** and create and develop a **World Language Support Tree**.

Our teacher colleagues are our first source of support. Our fellow teachers can be our best listeners – they can listen to our ideas about creativity and our plans to go on a creative journey. Explain to them what you are doing. Tell them you are starting to develop a **World Language Support Tree**. Tell them the tree will have varied leaves, including teacher colleagues, students, parents, administrators, community leaders, and yourself. Inform them that you would be honored to have them be a leaf on that support tree during your creative journey.

Our teacher colleagues can be a sounding board for our ideas. They can encourage the ideas or recommend a different approach to what you want to do. They can observe one of your classes and see the class in action as they participate in your new, creative classroom.

Ask them if they could meet with you one day a week after class for two weeks (two meetings) to discuss your new creative teaching strategies. Ask them what they envision to be the positives and negatives of these new creative strategies.

Ask them to be a world language cheerleader and visit your class the first day of your new creative class strategy. Ask your colleague to take a pictures of you with your class while they are involved in the new teaching strategy. On a second visit, have them do a cheer for your new ideas, then, have them make suggestions on how to improve your plan.

Take a picture of your colleague and put it onto a drawing you made on your bulletin board of the World Language Support Tree. Add photos throughout the year of all your helpers (leaves) who are part of your tree!

Note: Have your teacher colleagues complete the appropriate parts of the **Planner Support Page**. Be sure they use this **Rubric/Rating** during their participation of the creativity journey. This page is at the end of the human sources of support section for this chapter. You may choose to make a copy of that page to handout to teacher colleagues or send it digitally.

Why not have an end-of-the-year **World Language Support Tree** social/party for the teachers who have helped you throughout the year? Show them that you appreciate what they do for the kids and you. Provide them with a special food treat!

Human Sources of Support 2 – Students

Our students are our second source of support. Explain to them what you are doing. Tell them you are starting to develop a **World Language Support Tree**. Tell them the tree will have varied leaves, including teacher colleagues, students, parents, administrators, community leaders, and yourself. Inform them that you would be honored to have them be a leaf on that support tree during your creative journey. Let them know that you will be using various teaching strategies and ideas as you attempt to make learning more creative, fun, and exciting!

We can identify students to be our helpers in our creative endeavor and call these helpers **tutors** or **experts**. How many experts should there be in the class? Try to find a job for everyone, if possible. Select students in each class who could be tutors or experts in these categories: vocabulary, grammar, listening, speaking, reading, writing, sports, music, drama, singing, history, poetry, short stories, food, cooking, dance, art, painting, and entertainment. Throughout the year, they could assist you in setting up various creative projects. When you are doing small-group activities, selected experts could act as tutors and help the rest of the class.

Designate one group of three students to be helpers whenever you change your seating chart. They could move the desks. Another group of three students could be in charge of decorating the bulletin boards. Another small group could make signs – digitally or posters – to promote your new creativity strategies.

A couple of **cheerleaders** in each class could lead a cheer in the TL about your creative teaching strategies!

Take a picture of your student helpers. Include those along with your other support sources onto the **World Language Support Tree** drawing on your bulletin board!

Note: Have your students complete the appropriate parts of the **Planner Support Page**. Be sure they use this **Rubric/Rating** during their participation of the creativity journey. This page is at the end of the human sources of support section for this chapter. You may choose to make a copy of that page to handout to your students or send it digitally.

Why not have an end-of-the-year **World Language Support Tree** social/party for the students who have helped you throughout the year? Show them that you appreciate what they do and provide some easy-to-prepare native delicacy!

Human Sources of Support 3 – Parents

Our parents are our next source of support. Parents can be helpful in many ways. If we can get one parent in each of our classes to help us one day a month in this creative journey, we will have included parents as vital leaves on our **World Language Support Tree**. If we use the **World Language Support Tree**, other parents will want to be a part of this unique tree. They will be interested in getting involved in their child's world language learning experiences. They can be a **CHEERLEADER** for TL study in the community for they will now be active participants in the learning process!

First, we should explain to them what we are trying to do, that we want to make learning more fun for the students and for us. Explain to them that you want to change your teaching strategies. Ask them for their help in making your creative journey easier by giving advice to you and the students. Remember, they are parents and they understand their children well.

What can parents do? They can help with creative inspirations: parents can help us start and do a creative lesson plan by giving us their ideas. They can be a resource person and gather information for us, physically help set up new seating arrangements, and/or look for materials needed to do your creative lesson plan. They may be anxious to get the chance to show off their TL speaking and reading skills.

They can also help once the lesson has begun: They can watch and listen. They can decorate our bulletin boards. They can be class

photographer and take pictures of students in action. They can also be videographers and provide a video to us of our class in action. They can post information, photos, videos, and they can be cheerleaders for both the teacher and students.

Parents can also be great supporters of any spring or summer overseas trips you plan for your students. They can also be helpful when you take students on a local field trip. They may also want to chaperone these types of events.

Note: Have the parents complete the appropriate parts of the **Planner Support Page**. Be sure they use this **Rubric/Rating** during their participation of the creativity journey. This page is at the end of the human sources of support section for this chapter. You may choose to make a copy of that page to handout to parents or send it digitally.

Why not have an end-of-the-year **World Language Support Tree** social/party for the parents who have helped you throughout the year? Show them that you appreciate what they do for the kids and you. Provide some easy to prepare native cuisine for them. Give those parents a **WORLD LANGUAGE SUPPORT TREE CERTIFICATE OF APPRECIATION** for their help!

Human Sources of Support 4 – Administrators

Administrators are our fourth source of support as they form leaves on our **World Language Support Tree**. I include as administrators a wide array of school personnel. Let's include superintendents, principals, assistant principals, counselors, department chairs, the athletic director, the band director, the choir director, and the director of the school cafeteria.

The Superintendent: speak with the Superintendent and ask him/her to speak to one of your classes via Zoom. Ask him/her to speak about the importance of studying world languages. Ask him/her to speak about the positive aspects of your TL program.
The Principal: ask your Principal to be a cheerleader and visit two of your classes and do a cheer in the TL on the importance of studying a world language. The cheer should be short but one that encourages

students to study a language. Perhaps they could include a few words about their language study and world travel.

The Assistant Principal: speak with the Assistant Principal and see if he/she can dress up as a famous writer, painter, or athlete who came from a TL country. Have him/her give some words of advice to the students about studying a world language. Ask him/her to say a few sentences in the TL.

Counselor: ask the counselor to dress up and role-play the current president of a TL country. He/she is to speak about the importance of studying a world language in college, high school, middle school, and elementary school.

Department Chair: speak with a Department Chair of another department and ask him/her to speak to several of your classes about the link between her/his department and the world language department. This would involve the interdisciplinary connection that exists. What is the connection between world languages and social studies, science, or math?

Athletic Director: ask the AD to speak to some of your classes about an athlete who is now playing in professional sports. It could be a baseball, football, basketball, tennis, soccer, volleyball, swimmer, or golf star. Be sure the star is from a TL country.

Band Director: ask the band director to have some members of the band visit several of your classes and play a song native to a TL country! Ask the band director to speak about the history of the song. Introduce any band member who is currently in a world language class. Do this activity for an all-school World Language Day!

Choir Director: have the director of the school choir and some choir members sing a verse from a song in each of the world languages taught at your school. Have the choir sing over the school announcement system. Do the singing on an all-school World Language Day!

Director of School Cafeteria: have the director of the school kitchen prepare a meal or two native to the country where your languages are spoken. Do this for an all-school World Language Day.

Note: Have your administrators complete the appropriate parts of the **Planner Support Page**. Be sure they use this **Rubric/Rating** during

their participation of the creativity journey. This page is at the end of the human sources of support section for this chapter. You may choose to make a copy of that page to handout to the administrators or send it digitally.

Why not have an end-of-the-year **World Language Support Tree** social/party for the administrative leaders who have helped you throughout the year! Show them that you appreciate what they do for you and the kids. Provide some easy-to-prepare native desserts. Give those leaders a **WORLD LANGUAGE SUPPORT TREE CERTIFICATE OF APPRECIATION** (see Chapter 10) for their help!

Human Sources of Support 5 – Community

Our next source of support is our community. The area around the school, city, town, and neighborhoods may include doctors, lawyers, engineers, business professionals, small businesses, accountants, tech centers, dentists, veterinarians, optometrists, bakeries, pharmacies, restaurants, gym owners, hospitals, auto dealerships, auto repair shops, beauty salons, barbershops, clothing stores, theaters, bowling alleys, golf centers, ice cream shops, candy stores, airports, and colleges. And they may speak the TL or have traveled there and have valuable experiences to share.

Ask students or parents to help speak with TL-speaking community leaders. See if they can come to school and speak about the benefits of learning a world language. Invite native speakers in the community to speak about life in their native country. Ask the community leaders to help by being members – leaves – on the **World Language Support Tree**. They become leaves on the tree by helping you in your creative journey. Ask them to spend an hour a week with one class. Try to get several leaders helping at the same time, one for each class you have. What an experience to have a beautician, politician, athlete, singer, TV celebrity, journalist, doctor, dentist, shop owner, veterinarian, baker, pharmacist, gym owner, and restaurant owner all helping with your creative journey. Be sure to get photos of them to put onto your World Language Support Tree!

Here are some ideas and activities for the community leaders to help you in your creativity journey:

> **ACTFL:** Interpretive, Novice High; **CEFR:** A2+

- Decorate the room/bulletin boards.
- Speak to the class in the TL they took in high school.
- Help plan and teach a class.
- Relate why it is important to learn and know another language.
- Plan a photo shoot, allow the community leader to video or take photos of the class in action.
- Have the community leader speak about other countries he/she has visited, show pictures/video of visits.

> **ACTFL:** Interpretive, Novice High; **CEFR:** A2

- Lead a vocabulary day and teach students some important words of his/her/their profession – share both the English and world language words with the class.
- Ask the community leader if you can have a special class in his/her/their place of business.

> **ACTFL:** Presentational, Novice Mid; **CEFR:** A1

- Be a tutor and help students during a regular class.
- Be a world language **CHEERLEADER** and lead the class in a short TL cheer in the world language.

Community leaders can also be great supporters of any spring or summer overseas trips you plan for your students. Ask them if they could provide some financial assistance for student travel or for college scholarship assistance for worthy world language students.

> **ACTFL:** Presentational, Intermediate Mid; **CEFR:** A2+

- Community leaders can also be helpful when you take students on a local field trip. They may also want to chaperone these types of events. Visit their place of business. Have a student be the guide and speak in the world language!

Note: Have your community members complete the appropriate parts of the **Planner Support Page**. Be sure they use this **Rubric/Rating** during their participation of the creativity journey. This page is at the end of the human sources of support section for this chapter. You may choose to make a copy of that page to handout to the community members or send it digitally.

Have an end-of-the-year **World Language Support Tree** social/party for the community leaders who have helped you throughout the year. Show them that you appreciate what they do for you and the kids. Provide some easy-to-prepare native cuisine for them. Give those leaders a **WORLD LANGUAGE SUPPORT TREE CERTIFICATE OF APPRECIATION** for their help!

Human Sources of Support 6 – Myself

Our final source of support is ourselves. We must be a CHEERLEADER for ourselves, our class, and all others who are leaves on the World Language Support Tree. Yes, that means **you toot your own horn**! You are the most important branch and leaf of the World Language Support Tree. Without your efforts, there would be no tree.

We must publicize the **CREATIVE** things we do in class! Publicize special activities, using pictures and video clips of what we do in class. Show those to our classes and, if possible, share on acceptable social media sources as well as on school websites. Yes, we need to include ourselves on the World Language Support Tree because we are the **creators** of that tree! Let's put a large picture of **us** at the very top of the World Language Support Tree and let everyone know that we are on a CREATIVITY MISSION. Let's tell everyone we want to be **super creative** and then invite all your sources of support to be a part of the World Language Support Tree.

WE WANT TO HELP ALL OUR SOURCES OF SUPPORT TO BECOME MORE CREATIVE SO THEY CAN SHARE THOSE NEW CREATIVE IDEAS WITH OTHERS ON OUR WORLD LANGUAGE SUPPORT TREE.

Let's follow and use some of the creative ideas in this book!
YOU CAN MAKE THINGS HAPPEN!

Planner Support Page for Human Sources/Date _____

Please complete the answers below as well as the Rubric after you complete your task.

Sources of Support – Circle the support group you belong to and then answer the questions that follow. Be sure to complete the Rubric/Rating section at the bottom of this page.

Source of Support – Circle the one that pertains to you.

Teacher Colleague(s), Students, Parents, Administrators, Community, Myself

1. What did you do? What did you want the students in the world language class(es) to do? When did you do this and why?

   _____
   _____
   _____
   _____
   _____

2. What information and material did you need? Did you have all you needed to complete the task?

   _____
   _____
   _____
   _____
   _____

3. Did you complete your plan? Did you have fun? Did the students have fun?

   _____
   _____
   _____

4. **Rubric/Rating - Circle** your rating. How was your support experience in the world language classroom? Please answer the question that follows. **THANKS!**

   5 - outstanding, 4 - good, 3 - average, 4 - weak, 5 - terrible

How can I improve what I did? Would you like to help again? Why or why not?

_____
_____
_____
_____

Sources of Support 7 – Technology

Using Technology to Spark Creativity

Creativity and technology *do* work together, but in terms of creativity, we need to think of it less as playing games or watching videos and instead consider using it more like a tool. Technology has enabled creative teachers to explore new paths and imagine new possibilities. The COVID-19 pandemic has been a catalyst as well, first creating a need, providing a goal, and so many sites offered free memberships and tutoring that there has been an explosion of avenues opened. Surveys of students all agree: learning is more interesting when technology is involved.

There are several steps to go through before using technology. I personally use the SAMR method: do I want to **S**ubstitute, **A**ugment, **M**odify or **R**edefine an activity that I would like to do in a more creative way? That will depend on my goals: what should I do, and what should my students be able to do? Bloom's Digital Taxonomy (many examples can be found online) also has a great model to show ways to use technology instead of previous strategies.

Once goals are decided upon, proceed to examine the technology needs, and decide how much to spend, and if not free, where the money can be found to pay for it. I have been careful to include only free resources in this chapter. Another issue is availability: check with your technology team to see if a site is allowed or blocked on your students' devices, or to get it whitelisted so they can use it. You don't want any nasty surprises, such as spending time making a stupendous presentation only to find out they can't see it or use it in the way you'd like it to be used.

But first, you need the creative idea. Here are several pages of resources and suggestions:

Social Media for Ideas on Presentation and Collaboration

The first way technology can aid with creativity is by giving us the opportunity to view others' creativity, and for creative teachers to share (and even market) their own. These opportunities occur mostly through social media: Facebook, Instagram, blogs, YouTube, and others.

BLOGS AND PODCASTS

Both of these are forms of social media used for networking. Which one to choose mostly depends on if you prefer reading or listening to discussions and information on teaching a TL.

A blog is designed for reading. Blog entries are organized like a diary and posted on a website. On a blog, teachers can talk about anything they want, interview others, play music, and share struggles and successes. All it takes is access to a photo or video recording device to make your own blog. You can vent about a topic or situation, engage in online discussions, and share creative ideas on social media platforms, which are usually read on a computer. Blogs enable us to post whatever we want and comment on it or receive comments from colleagues, but not in real time. Feedback may come quickly or slowly as readers access your blog when they have time.

How often do you need to blog? Most teachers only blog when they are moved to share something. Your audience is whatever you choose: fellow educators, students, and parents.

Reading someone else's blog is great if you feel stuck or need a mentor, too. Some free sites for creating teacher blogs are Edublogs.org, Blogger.com (managed by Google), Wix.com, and Wordpress.com. I suggest you find and follow a few bloggers to get your creativity stimulated by what others are doing. Some examples are listed here (there are MANY more to be found):

Spanish

www.funforspanishteachers.com For preschool and elementary level teachers.

https://www.fluentu.com/blog/educator-spanish/ For middle school and high school levels.

http://palmyraspanish1.blogspot.com/ Comprehensible input (CI) ideas from three teachers.
https://www.creativelanguageclass.com/ Two teachers share creative ideas since 2012.
https://srojeda.com/ For advanced classes.

French

https://thefrenchcorner.net/ By a middle school teacher.
https://www.fluentu.com/blog/educator-french/ A collection of blogs from French teachers.

Multiple Languages

The Motivated Classroom on Apple Podcasts my personal favorite, both theory and practical suggestions.
https://language-gym.com/ French, Italian, German, Spanish and more.
https://wlclassroom.com/ World Language Classroom collaboration site.

A podcast is designed for listening; it is only audio. Podcasts can be listened to on a variety of devices. Podcasts encourage speaking skills in the teacher and listening skills in whoever listens. Podcasts can be motivational monologues, interviews, or even online courses where new skills are taught. Because podcasts are audio, you can also hear sarcasm or irony, humor, and intelligence or knowledge in the speaker's voice, as well as intonation and accent if a native speaker has made it.

Podcasts generally are done on some sort of schedule, so people know when to tune in to a new one; many are weekly or monthly.

How does a podcast spark creativity? This book is a good example, as it is due to a discussion authors Tom and Deb had on Tom's podcast, World Language Café: https://podcasts.apple.com/us/podcast/toms-world-language-cafe/id1366590907

Other Podcasts to Check Out

https://podcasts.apple.com/us/podcast/preaching-to-acquire/id1487871072 Using CI techniques.

https://www.liamprinter.com/podcast.html The Motivated Classroom: theory and low prep tips.
https://weteachlang.com/ We Teach Languages is a collaborative podcast from several people.

Spanish

https://www.lamaestraloca.com/podcast/ Teaching La Vida Loca.
https://www.newsinslowspanish.com/latino News in easy Spanish.

French

https://coffeebreaklanguages.com/coffeebreakfrench/ Comes with accompanying notes.
https://www.sbs.com.au/language/english/podcast/sbs-easy-french News in easy French.

What types of things could you do creatively by using a blog or podcast? Choose a topic you want to know more about, research it, and share it in an easy-to-read format. Tell stories about places you have been or topics or people you find interesting. Critique books you have read or movies you've seen. Interview teachers and authors you find inspiring. Talk about challenges you have faced and how you handled them. Share games or units you have created or found that your students really liked. Ask for suggestions on a unit you have created, or a problem you are having. Interview someone in your field that you admire or would like to know better. Really, any topic is appropriate for a blog.

FACEBOOK, TWITTER, AND MORE
There are many teacher groups on social media where ideas and resources are shared, questions are asked and answered, and new creations can be posted and tested for comments and suggestions. On Facebook alone right now, there are language-specific groups, textbook-specific groups, teaching method-specific groups (such as CI, teaching proficiency through reading and storytelling, and more), groups for finding pen pals and exchanges, tech groups for language

teachers, country-specific groups (great for culture), autobiographical, cultural and advice sites written by natives overseas or by Americans living abroad, groups devoted to TL music, art, films….and I am still finding new ones.

Twitter has been very popular with teachers, and there are quite a few teacher groups that meet regularly. On Twitter, I can search by hashtag in English or my TL and find postings to use with students (such as a list of "When I was little, I believed…" or ways to express love to use for Valentine's Day, phrases that use colors, weather expressions, etc.) and there are discussion groups to find as well. I recommend #langchat where they do book reading groups and lots of other topics, and #mfltwitterati where web workshops and many resources are shared. I set up a private Twitter group for my students where I can have them post pictures ("post a photo of your breakfast" for class discussion that day), answer or ask questions, and I can post things for them to read. I also post photos of classroom activities for parents who follow the site.

Other social media sites with large numbers of teachers actively contributing are Instagram, Pinterest, and LinkedIn. Instagram is like Twitter but more picture focused. Pinterest is a place to collect useful sites on topics of interest. LinkedIn is for communicating with other professionals in your subject area as well as career oriented.

Creating Content

Another way technology aids in creativity is that it provides the ability to enhance the creative process by presenting new platforms for the creativity to exist on (and come from), for example, to create beautiful, impactful documents, posters, etc., for use in our classrooms and in presentations for students.

VISUAL CONTENT

Having a visually stimulating and attractive presentation can greatly enhance your students' participation in an activity. Let your inner artist fly when you create a Bitmoji classroom of reading or listening activities or a funny avatar to introduce the day's lesson, a meme about your expectations for a project or your class rules, instructions for the day they

will have a substitute teacher, and more. Avatars are easy to create! You can make one that looks like you (https://www.bitmoji.com/), branch out and be a talking animal or classroom object (https://blabberize.com/), or a famous person, alien, or another option (https://l-www.voki.com/).

Some free options (though most have paid upgrades available) for making visuals, which I have used and enjoy, include:

Canva and Adobe CCE are both exactly what you need to create your blog, but they have many other uses as well. Canva (https://www.canva.com/) works with any sort of web browser and helps streamline the process of making a visual: thousands of templates plus access to lots of photos (or edit your own) to produce (TL if desired) newsletters, brochures, posters, presentations and videos, certificates, Instagram posts, calendars, storyboards, class schedules, and much more. If using this for collaboration, Canva is preferable to Adobe CCE, and in my opinion, it is easier for beginners.

Adobe Creative Cloud Express (https://www.adobe.com/express/) offers the same sort of experience as Canva (thousands of templates and royalty-free images) and works on a mobile phone as well as a computer. It is the best for exporting and editing images (especially removing backgrounds) and for professional things like resumes.

Piktochart (https://piktochart.com) is easy to use to make many sorts of visuals: you can spend a lot of time on the previous two browsing; Piktochart is more focused on sharing data via infographics, charts, graphs, and timelines, but also offers video editing and an image selection.

Infographics present information (class rules, survey results, cultural data) in colorful, eye-catching form easy enough for even beginners to interpret. Creations made are then easy to imbed in a blog or class website, too. Infographics are not only effective, they are easy: it takes about 30 minutes to make one. My favorite is Piktochart (see above), but other great free sites for making infographics are: Canva, (https://www.canva.com/create/infographics/), Visme (https://www.visme.co/make-infographics/), and Easel.ly (https://www.easel.ly/).

I also often use PicMonkey (https://www.picmonkey.com/) for photo editing.

I have not used but have heard about these as well: Stencil (getstencil.com) focuses on being simple to use; Snappa (https://snappa.com) lets you post directly to the Internet without leaving Snappa, but the free plan is limited; Pixlr X (https://pixlr.com/) is very much like Canva.

STORYTELLING TOOLS

Students today seem more resistant to reading, so the more attractive we can make the reading, the better. Storytelling also is great for introducing vocabulary and sentence structure, so no matter what you want to teach, this is a useful strategy and a great place to exercise your creativity.

Visual creativity in storytelling

Since stories begin by introducing characters, why not use a fake Facebook page, or a site for creating fake texts between people? The Classtools site (https://www.classtools.net/FB/home-page) has a free Fakebook creator, as well as other activities. I have seen fake text messages made into huge posters in museums, with simulated conversations on historical and artistic topics. I like to create conversations to review the plot in books we are reading, and have students guess who wrote the texts. The fake text message site (https://ifaketextmessage.com/tutorial/) provides a tutorial.

Another way to grab students' interest immediately is by using cartoons, storyboards, or videos. What is the difference between a storyboard and a cartoon? Very little: a storyboard is for conveying information, such as a summary of past topics or an introduction to a new one. Cartoons have a more humor-and-entertainment purpose. Popular sites for creating these are:

Canva: https://www.canva.com/comic-strips/templates/Has ready-made templates you can modify to your taste.
MakeBeliefsComix: https://makebeliefscomix.com/comic-strip-starters/ Why not do an "All About Me" comic to introduce yourself to students at the beginning of the year? MakeBeliefsComix has characters,

backgrounds, objects and other elements to assemble into two- to four-panel strips as you wish.

Pixton: https://app.pixton.com/#/edu Has both an avatar builder and a comic creator, plus tutorials, but is more artistic than the other sites: instead of preset characters, you can customize yours by adjusting face, hair, body, clothing, etc., and upload photos from Google and any creative commons visual, or your own computer. The free version is only for a short time, and then a subscription is required.

Storyboard That: https://www.storyboardthat.com/storyboard-creator A free site with backgrounds already created and ready to populate to retell events and reinforce reading comprehension.

Powtoon: https://www.powtoon.com/edu-home/ To make video cartoons, I like Powtoon, where there are hundreds of templates to choose from. It is fun to put real people's heads onto a cartoon body, and then upload the final product onto sites like EdPuzzle.

Prezi: https://prezi.com/education/ Another good option for creating gallery walks (that look like an actual museum, but don't have to be anything about art or history) as well as videos. It is also available both online and offline.

Storybird: https://storybird.com/membership-educator If you'd like your story to look just like a book, with pages that turn, try Storybird. While making, sharing, and reading are free, downloading or printing charge a fee.

Puppet Pals on the Apple App Store and Sock Puppets for iPads actually will lip sync with the speaker's voice and are hugely entertaining as well as great listening practice. Also fun, especially for younger students, are some apps for making stories with animation and audio, which are discussed next.

Audiovisual (Narrated) creativity in storytelling

Adding audio to pictures engages even more of a student's brain. I have used the Slidestory app (available from Apple's App Store), Storybird (https://www.storybird.com/educators), which charges a fee after a trial period, and Voicethread (https://voicethread.com/) to add audio to slides (Voicethread has a free subscription, but it is limited to just a few slides). Voicethread is even interactive: you or others can ask and

answer questions using text or audio – great for communicating with pen pals! But you can also add audio to any Google Slides or Canva slide show. Introduce your students to your family, your favorite sport, or leisure activity, show photos from a trip, and more.

AUDIO CREATIVITY

FlipGrid: https://info.flipgrid.com/ A great tool for social learning (speaking and communication). It has been the only site I've used since I was introduced to it. It is incredibly easy to use. You can post a question to answer, a video (yours or from the Internet) to watch, and even simulate a discussion. You can place stickers and disguises on yourself, embed it, or assign watching it.

INTERACTIVE CLASSWORK

PearDeck: www.peardeck.com Will take any worksheets or slide shows and make them interactive to rock your classroom. There are five free uploads, but it offers unlimited creation on the site. Then, add multiple choice or open-ended quiz questions, polls, draw-an-image or draggable practice, attach videos, audio, or links to other websites.

Jamboard: https://jamboard.google.com/ An online whiteboard by Google where students and teacher can draw and add text and images for everyone to view and share input. It allows students and teacher to interact in real time and share materials and notes instantly.

Padlet: https://padlet.com/ An online site where students can place their work for everyone to view and leave comments. Recently, I managed a Padlet where students and teachers from thousands of schools and 14 different countries contributed memes about music. It was easy to set up and moderate, and a lot of fun. I also use Padlet for my students to post "shame photos" to practice the past tense ("I ate a whole pie") and to post their wanted photos to apply to join my pirate crew.

ThingLink: https://www.thinglink.com/ A Thinglink is an image with dots placed on it. Each dot is a link to a text, a video, a practice activity, a quiz, a survey, a photo, an audio selection, or anything else you can think of. I have made Thinglinks to introduce my students

to sites in Paris, to link cultural videos, music, etc. to a photo of the poster from a movie we are watching, or to create a site to practice a grammar skill. Using a Thinglink is somewhat like opening a door on an advent calendar: you never know what a dot may lead you to, and students appreciate the anticipatory mystery.

GAMES

Using elements that make video games fun, you can present information in a format (point scoring, strategizing, team competition) that will keep them engaged in learning the TL.

Remember scavenger hunts? There are apps, but our tech team has blocked all of them (most are on Google Play). It is so easy to do your own online, though. All you need is the Internet, a list of items to look for (a blue jacket, a small ball) and photograph OR info to find online. Organize some teams, share the list in a group chat or email (or on a Padlet!), set a time limit, and begin!

Escape rooms are all the rage; why not do an escape game online? Room Escape Maker https://roomescapemaker.com/ features virtual rooms you can customize with questions on content for the unit being studied, or any other topic you may choose. Students click on items in the room to read texts, watch videos, or study images to get the answers to put on an online form (I use Google forms) to unlock a series of locks to "escape." These take some planning, but once that is set, they are easy to create. Google has a helpful set of instructions and suggestions at https://sites.google.com/view/creatingonlineers/create-your-own.

Choose Your Own Adventure games are also very addictive. In this, readers will begin a story but then be faced with a choice between action A and action B. Each choice will take them to a different event, with a different conclusion. I have students storyboard as they read, or write down "their" story, or read two or three versions and summarize their favorite (orally or in written form). First, plan the story and all the directions it would take, and then use Google Slides or Google Forms (there are YouTube videos that will walk you through the creation steps) or Text Adventures (https://textadventures.co.uk/quest) to create the adventure.

Using technology is a type of creative endeavor that your students will applaud and enjoy.

Planning Page for Using Technology

UNIT OR LESSON: _____

What I'd like to do more creatively (circle):

introduce   practice   product   assess

GOAL: Students should be able to: _____

Sites I've found to use:

_____ Free   or $_____

_____ Free   or $_____

_____ Free   or $_____

NOW, choose one of the sites.

Have I tried the site after signing in as a student?   Yes   No

Was it blocked?   Yes   No

What technology will be required? _____

New skills I may have to teach students in order to use this: _____

Pros of the site: _____

Cons of the site: _____

Is support easily available? _____

How hard will this be to grade/assess? _____

REFLECTION

What went well? What suggestions did students make for changes? What will you do differently next time?

9

The Path of Persistence
Creative Evaluation/How Did You Do?

Introduction

Persistence is necessary for any creative endeavor. Creative people need to encourage creativity and overcome difficulties or failure through **persistence** to continue to be creative. After a presentation of the importance of **being persistent** in your march to creativity, there are some **super-creative ideas** on how to keep going when things get challenging. This chapter closes with a group of **self-assessment cards** that allow you **to focus on details and rate** the good and the not-so-good of your creative endeavors. **What were your successes? What were your failures**? Did you learn from your failures? What will be next? These cards provide you with ideas to help focus on the present, past, and what you can do in the future to improve what happens on your creativity journey.

Self-assessment cards include these topics: Your Persistence, Your New Creative Teaching Strategies, Your Support Groups, Your Expectations, Your Newest Super-Creative Teaching Strategies, Your Successes, Your Failures, Your Positivity, and Rewarding Others. **Please feel free to print copies of the cards.**

DOI: 10.4324/9781003293255-10

Not every idea you have will work; failure is part of the process of creativity. As Joseph Chilton Pearce said, "To live a creative life, we must lose our fear of being wrong." This is why persistence is such an important part of any creativity. You need to be willing to adjust or abandon the ideas that don't work and keep trying. Persistence helps overcome failure due to bad luck, lack of resources, and all possible excuses for not trying something new.

Historically, the famous innovators didn't quit; instead, they took a break from the focus on the troublesome issue (such as a temporary lack of creative ideas, or a snag in implementation) and did something else. I recommend daydreaming or something routine and boring like folding laundry or other chores, or something pleasant like cuddling with a pet or taking a bubble bath. While the conscious mind is taking a break and (hopefully) relaxing, the subconscious is still working on a solution, and often finds one and possibly a few new ideas as well. We have probably all heard of someone having an inspiration just before falling asleep; this is a good illustration of that phenomenon.

But persistence isn't only for the idea-forming part of the process. Creative people like you constantly think of ways to improve the creation, leading to other creations.

Here are some ways to encourage persistence:

- Sharing your interests with others.
- Injecting fun into work that interests you.
- Rewarding small achievements by doing something you like (music, a movie, food, etc.).
- Rewarding the *creative process*, not the outcome, no matter what the results are.
- Showing your work even if not perfect; don't wait for the ideal time.
- Seeking feedback from different points of view.
- Breaking activities and preparations down into smaller, manageable bits.
- Stating your goal and creating a daily or weekly plan to achieve it.
- Putting a visual reminder of your objective somewhere you'll see it a lot.
- Using a journal to keep track of progress made.
- Not procrastinating (or quitting!).

If your idea fails, persist and perhaps even find a new idea by:

- Moving to a new place.
- Learning more about the topic.
- Finding a solution to part of the problem instead of looking for one that solves everything.
- Switching back and forth between two projects or ideas (taking a brief break from one while working on the other, but NO multitasking).
- Trying a different strategy next time.
- Examining the causes of the failure.
- Writing "I can do this" and putting it somewhere you'll see it a lot.
- Thinking about the problem as if it happened to someone else or an animal, superhero, etc., or in a different time or place (use your imagination).

Burnout will occur if (and these are things you should NOT do):

- You expect too much of yourself. It is okay to take a break when tired, upset, etc.
- You give yourself homework. This should be FUN and if it isn't, rethink or re-examine your goal(s).
- You set the bar higher for each successive idea or activity.
- You set an unreasonable time limit to accomplish a goal.
- You try to come up with a specific number of ideas; just let whatever comes to be enough.
- You work to solve problems that have no solution possible.

> **Self-Assessment Card 1 – My Persistence**
>
> 1. Were you persistent enough in your efforts to be more creative? Why or why not? _____
>
> 2. How can you be less persistent? More persistent? _____
>
> 3. What good things happened when you were persistent? _____
>
> 4. How can you improve your persistence with any future projects? _____
>
> 5. What plan do you want to create for yourself to improve your persistence? _____
>
> **Rating for How Your Persistence Turned Out**
>
> Circle the best answer.
>
> Excellent   Good   So, so   Not good   Awful

Copyright material from Deborah Blaz and Tom Alsop (2023), *Sparking Creativity in the World Language Classroom: Strategies and Ideas to Build Your Students' Language Skills,* Routledge.

Self-Assessment Card 2 – Your New Creative Teaching Strategies

1. Did you develop some creative and new teaching strategies? Which ones? _____
2. How did the new teaching strategies turn out? Why? _____
3. Did students like the new strategies? Why or why not?
   _____
   _____

4. Do you plan to use some of the new strategies again in the future? Why or why not?
   _____
   _____

5. How can you improve what you did? _____
   _____

6. Which new teaching strategy was the easiest to do?
   _____
   Why? _____
7. Which new teaching strategy that you tried was the most creative, and why? _____
   _____

8. What good things happened when you used the new creative teaching strategy(ies)?
   _____
   Why? _____

Rating for How Your New Creative Strategies Turned Out
Circle the best answer.

Excellent   Good   So, so   Not good   Awful

Copyright material from Deborah Blaz and Tom Alsop (2023), *Sparking Creativity in the World Language Classroom: Strategies and Ideas to Build Your Students' Language Skills,* Routledge.

Self-Assessment Card 3 – Your Support System

1. Who supported your creative plans the most? Students, parents, colleagues, administrators, community, yourself? _____
   Why? _____
   _____

   How? _____
   _____

2. Which group supported you the least? Why and when?
   _____
   _____

3. What did the support groups do to help you be more creative?
   _____
   _____

4. Was it worth having the support? Why?
   _____
   _____

5. How did you organize the support helpers?
   _____
   _____

6. How can you improve your support from others for new projects?
   _____
   _____

Rating for How Your Support Turned Out
Circle the best answer.

Excellent   Good   So, so   Not good   Awful

Copyright material from Deborah Blaz and Tom Alsop (2023), *Sparking Creativity in the World Language Classroom: Strategies and Ideas to Build Your Students' Language Skills,* Routledge.

Self-Assessment Card 4 – Your Newest Super-Creative Teaching Strategies

Note: This newest super-creative teaching strategy is more creative than your super-creative strategy on Assessment Card 2. This newest super-creative teaching strategy is in rarified air!

1. What was your new super-creative teaching strategy?
   _____
   _____

2. How and when did you do this super-creative teaching strategy?
   _____
   _____

3. Did your students like your super-creative teaching strategy? Explain a bit.
   _____

4. Did you feel better after being super creative with your new teaching strategy? _____
   Why or why not? _____
   _____
   _____

5. What are some ideas to help you find and try another super-creative teacher strategy in the future? _____
   _____
   _____

6. What is your favorite super-creative teaching strategy? Why? _____
   _____
   _____

7. How and when will you do your next super-creative teaching strategy?
   _____

Rating for How Your Super-Creative Idea Turned Out

Circle the best answer.

Excellent   Good   So, so   Not good   Awful

Copyright material from Deborah Blaz and Tom Alsop (2023), *Sparking Creativity in the World Language Classroom: Strategies and Ideas to Build Your Students' Language Skills,* Routledge.

> **Self-Assessment Card 5 – Your Expectations**
>
> 1. Were your expectations too high, just right, or too low during your creative journey? Why? _____
>
> 2. Did your expectations make you tired? Why? _____
>
> 3. Did your expectations help your students learn? Why? _____
>
> 4. How can you improve your expectations to make them more doable in the future? _____
>
> 5. What good things happened when your expectations were just right? Why? _____
>
> 6. What expectations did your students have as they took part in the march toward more creativity in the world language classroom? ___
>
>   Why? _____
>
> 7. Do you see more creativity in what you and your students are doing now versus before?
>   _____
>
> **Rating for How Your Expectations Turned Out**
>
> Circle the best answer.
>
> Excellent   Good   So, so   Not good   Awful

Copyright material from Deborah Blaz and Tom Alsop (2023), *Sparking Creativity in the World Language Classroom: Strategies and Ideas to Build Your Students' Language Skills*, Routledge.

Self-Assessment Card 6 – Your Successes

1. Did you have lots of successes on your creative journey? When? Why?
   _____
   _____
   _____

2. Did you have more successes than failures? Why?
   _____
   _____

3. What brought you the most successes on your creative journey?
   _____
   Why? _____
4. How did you feel when you were successful? _____
5. What good things happened when you were successful? _____
   _____
   _____

6. What do you need to do to have more successes? _____
   _____
   _____

7. How can you better share your successes with others? _____
   _____
   Why? _____

Rating for How Your Successes Turned Out

Circle the best answer.

Excellent   Good   So, so   Not good   Awful

Copyright material from Deborah Blaz and Tom Alsop (2023), *Sparking Creativity in the World Language Classroom: Strategies and Ideas to Build Your Students' Language Skills*, Routledge.

Self-Assessment Card 7 – Your Failures

1. On your creative journey did you have lots of failures, some, or a few? Why?
   _____
   _____

2. How can you reduce the number of failures?
   _____
   _____

3. Did you learn a lot from your failures? What? _____
   _____

4. Were there levels of failure? Which failures were the worst, average, and least?
   _____
   _____

5. What good things happened when you failed?
   _____
   _____

6. How did you use a failure to do better the next time?
   _____
   _____

7. What is the most important thing you learned when you failed? How can you improve how not to fail in the future? _____
   _____
   _____

8. How did failure help you with your successes?
   _____

Rating for How Your Failures Turned Out

Circle the best answer.

Excellent   Good   So, so   Not good   Awful

Self-Assessment Card 8 – Your Positivity

1. Was I positive enough in most of my efforts to be more creative? Why or why not?
   _____
   _____

2. How can I be more positive in the future? In what ways and how?
   _____
   _____

3. Did you influence colleagues with your positivity? How?
   _____
   _____

4. Did you influence your students with your positivity? How?
   _____

5. What good things happened when you were positive?
   _____
   _____

6. How did you reward students' positivity? Why?
   _____

7. Did you reward your positivity? Why?_____
   _____

8. Did you have a **Let's Be Super Positive Day** for your classes? Why?
   _____
   _____
   _____

9. What was your most positive moment during your creative journey?
   _____
   _____

Rating for How Your Positivity Turned Out

Circle the best answer.

Excellent   Good   So, so   Not good   Awful

Copyright material from Deborah Blaz and Tom Alsop (2023), *Sparking Creativity in the World Language Classroom: Strategies and Ideas to Build Your Students' Language Skills,* Routledge.

Self-Assessment Card 9 – Rewarding Others

1. Did you give your students enough awards? _____
   What awards and for what reason? _____
   _____

2. What rewards were the most popular with your students? _____
   _____
   Why? _____
   _____

3. Did you give any recognition awards to your Principal, Assistant Principal, teacher colleagues, and department chairpersons for their support of world language study and your creativity journey?
   _____
   _____
   What recognition awards? _____
   _____

4. Did you give your parents a recognition award? What and why? _____
   _____
   _____

5. What good things happened when you recognized others? _____
   _____
   _____

6. Did you recognize community members with awards for their support of world languages? How and why? _____
   _____

7. What plans do you have to improve your recognition of others in the future? _____
   _____
   _____

Rating for How Your Rewarding Others Turned Out

Circle the best answer.

Excellent   Good   So, so   Not good   Awful

Copyright material from Deborah Blaz and Tom Alsop (2023), *Sparking Creativity in the World Language Classroom: Strategies and Ideas to Build Your Students' Language Skills,* Routledge.

10

My Creativity Recipe Cards

Introduction

This chapter contains Creativity Recipe Cards. Each recipe contains portions of the Six Steps to Success at being creative: a touch of curiosity, a dash of imagination, creativity, goal-setting, implementation, and evaluation, on a wide variety of topics that apply to any world language.

The purpose of the recipe cards is to make it fun for you to prepare classes. You can use the recipe cards when you want to crank up your inner creativity. The cards help create situations in which the students get to work in groups, interact, and do lots of fun communicative activities and play games, etc. while learning their language. The goal is to let the students use their TL while they participate in the recipe.

There are 22 categories of cards with three recipes (A, B, C) for each category. A cards are Appetizers, B cards are Main Courses, and C cards are Desserts – 66 cards in all. Recipes are organized into appropriate levels of language learning. There are ten recipes for Level 1, six for Level 2, and six for the Advanced Level. There is also a set of card templates the reader may use to create her/his own recipes.

The recipes are divided into levels. In each level, there are cards for vocabulary, grammar, and culture. Level 1 has six vocabulary recipes, two grammar recipes, and two recipes for culture. Level 2 and the

Advanced Level each have two vocabulary recipes, two grammar recipes, and two recipes for culture.

Level 1 vocabulary includes greetings, clothing, weather, food, and more. Level 1 grammar uses the verb "to have" and more. Level 1 culture includes Christmas carols and more.

Level 2 vocabulary includes a shopping spree and more. Level 2 grammar focuses on commands and more. Level 2 culture includes dance and more.

The Advanced Level vocabulary includes hospital and more. Advanced grammar focuses on the present subjunctive and more. Advanced culture includes poet's day and more.

Enjoy using the 22 recipes as needed throughout the school year. If you like to cook, use these recipes **often.** There are templates for Creativity Recipe Cards at the end for you to use for creating **your own** TL creativity recipes. **HAVE FUN!**

Celebrate the creative chef inside you. For added fun, **wear a chef's hat** when you use the recipe card so the kids know you are trying out a new recipe **From the kitchen of (your name)!** Explain to them the ingredients, how to prepare them, how long it will take, how to serve, and what the results will be. Using a short, on-card rating, ask them if they liked the appetizer, main course, and dessert. Have the students make their own chef's hat and wear them as well.

DO IT! Enjoy the recipes. **CELEBRATE** your renewed **POSITIVITY. HAVE FUN!**

LEVEL 1 – RECIPES 1–10

Vocabulary: Recipes 1–6
Grammar: Recipes 7–8
Culture: Recipes 9–10

Alphabet – Creativity Recipe Card 1

1A-Appetizer

Ingredients
A handout with the letters of the phonetical alphabet as they are orally said in the language or the letters listed on a smart board or white board. You can also share the digital file with students to use on their tablets or laptops.

How to do
Give handout to the students or project and review letters on the smart board, white board, or digital files (tablets, laptops). Orally repeat the letters with the entire class. Next, break up the class and put them in pairs. Have them practice and repeat the letters in pairs.

ACTFL: Interpersonal, Novice Low; **CEFR:** A1

Time to do
10 minutes
Serves 1 to 30 students

Results
Who liked this appetizer? (Circle the response to this recipe.)

Everyone   almost everyone

some   none

From the kitchen of _____

Copyright material from Deborah Blaz and Tom Alsop (2023), *Sparking Creativity in the World Language Classroom: Strategies and Ideas to Build Your Students' Language Skills*, Routledge.

1B-Main Course

Ingredients
Prepare a list of 50 words in the TL that are fairly short. Have a difficult list of 20 words that you can use to do the final elimination. Make a certificate in your world language or a button or star for the champion speller.

ACTFL: Interpersonal, Novice Low; **CEFR:** A1

How to do
Have all students stand while you repeat the word twice. Students are then to spell the word phonetically in the TL. The last student left standing is the Champion Speller of the Class!

Time to do
30 minutes
Serves 2 to 30 students

Results
Who liked this main course? (Circle the response to this recipe.)

Everyone   almost everyone

some   none

From the kitchen of _____

Copyright material from Deborah Blaz and Tom Alsop (2023), *Sparking Creativity in the World Language Classroom: Strategies and Ideas to Build Your Students' Language Skills,* Routledge.

1C-Dessert

Ingredients
A handout with the letters of the phonetical alphabet as they are orally spoken in the language or the letters listed onto a smart board or white board. You can also share the digital file with students to use on their pads or laptops.

How to do
Have an alphabet dictation game called *Say the Word Aloud*. Students are to raise their hand and give the correct word that you have just read to the class in the phonetical alphabet of the language. Have a student keep score. Name the winner the Alphabet Star of the Day. Take a picture of the winner and put the picture onto the bulletin board!

ACTFL: Interpersonal, Novice Low; **CEFR:** A1

Time to do
15 minutes
Serves 1 to 30 students

Results
Who liked this dessert? (Circle the response to this recipe.)

Everyone   almost everyone

some   none

From the kitchen of _____

Copyright material from Deborah Blaz and Tom Alsop (2023), *Sparking Creativity in the World Language Classroom: Strategies and Ideas to Build Your Students' Language Skills*, Routledge.

Greetings-Farewells – Creativity Recipe Card 2

2A-Appetizer

Ingredients
Prepare a list of common greeting and farewells in your TL. Include as many as you can. Include greetings from your textbook.

ACTFL: Interpersonal, Novice Low; **CEFR:** A1

How to do
Make copies and hand out or present the greetings and farewells onto a document camera or digitally onto a smart board or white board. Have the class practice the greeting aloud and then work in pairs to practice the greetings.

Time to do
15 minutes
Serves 1 to 30 students

Results
Who liked this appetizer? (Circle the response to this recipe.)

Everyone   almost everyone

some   none

From the kitchen of _____

Copyright material from Deborah Blaz and Tom Alsop (2023), *Sparking Creativity in the World Language Classroom: Strategies and Ideas to Build Your Students' Language Skills*, Routledge.

2B-Main Course

Ingredients
Use the list of words (greetings and farewells) from the Appetizer card. Have a prize for the winning trio of students. The prize could be a star, button, sticker, candy, etc.

How to do
Make copies and hand out or present the greetings/farewells onto a document camera or digitally on a smart board or white board. Have the class practice the greeting aloud and then work in pairs and present a short skit using at least six greetings. Students are to work in groups of three. Have students present their short skit to the class. Award a prize to the best trio of presenters!

ACTFL: Interpersonal, then presentational, Novice Low; **CEFR:** A1

Time to do
25 minutes
Serves 3 to 30 students

Results
Who liked this main course? (Circle the response to this recipe.)

Everyone   almost everyone

some   none

From the kitchen of _____

2C-Dessert

Ingredients
Use the list of words (greetings and farewells) from the Appetizer card. Give a prize to the winning trio of students. Prize could be a star, button, sticker, candy, etc. Scramble the letters in ten greetings/farewells. Write ten words with missing letters. Use both of these in the two games listed in the **HOW TO DO** section immediately following.

ACTFL: Presentational, Novice Low; **CEFR:** A1

How to do
Scramble some of the greetings and farewells in your TL. Students are to unscramble the words and say the word aloud in the world language. Follow this quick-hitting activity with the Fill the Blank game. Students are to say the word aloud in their TL after filling the missing letters of the word. Have a student keep score.

Time to do
15 minutes
Serves 1 to 30 students

Results
Who liked this dessert? (Circle the response to this recipe.)

Everyone   almost everyone

some   none

From the kitchen of _____

Copyright material from Deborah Blaz and Tom Alsop (2023), *Sparking Creativity in the World Language Classroom: Strategies and Ideas to Build Your Students' Language Skills*, Routledge.

Weather Expressions – Creativity Recipe Card 3

3A-Appetizer

Ingredients
Prepare a list of common expressions of weather in your TL. These expressions can come from your textbook or from an online list of weather expressions found after searching the Internet.

How to do
Hand out the list of weather expressions to the students or list the weather expressions onto the smart board, white board, or digital files (tablets, laptops). You can also have students do an online search for TL weather expressions. The students then practice repeating the weather expressions in pairs. Have students act out the weather expressions in pairs.

> **ACTFL:** Presentational, Novice Low; **CEFR:** A1

Time to do
15 minutes
Serves 2 to 30 students

Results
Who liked this appetizer? (Circle the response to this recipe.)

Everyone   almost everyone

some   none

From the kitchen of _____

Copyright material from Deborah Blaz and Tom Alsop (2023), *Sparking Creativity in the World Language Classroom: Strategies and Ideas to Build Your Students' Language Skills*, Routledge.

3B-Main Course

Ingredients
Use your list of weather expressions from the Appetizer card. Award prizes to the best weather forecast pair. Allow pairs to dress up and act the role of TV meteorologists!

> **ACTFL:** Presentational, Novice Mid; **CEFR:** A1

How to do
Students are to play the role of meteorologist. Have them work in pairs and create a weather forecast for their nightly TV show in the world language for today and tomorrow's weather. Award Oscars to the best weather skits! Take pictures of the winning pair and use on the bulletin board.

Time to do
25 minutes
Serves 2 to 30 students

Results
Who liked this main course? (Circle the response to this recipe.)

Everyone   almost everyone

some   none

From the kitchen of _____

Copyright material from Deborah Blaz and Tom Alsop (2023), *Sparking Creativity in the World Language Classroom: Strategies and Ideas to Build Your Students' Language Skills,* Routledge.

3C-Dessert

Ingredients
Use the original weather expressions list. Have prizes for the winning team. Prepare five weather expressions for each team to act out.

How to do
Play charades. Divide the class into two teams. Each team gets a point for guessing the weather expression that is acted out by someone from their team. Have a student keep score. Award a night of free homework!

ACTFL: Interpersonal, Novice Low; **CEFR:** A1

Time to do
20 minutes
Serves 1 to 30 students

Results
Who liked this dessert? (Circle the class response to this recipe.)

Everyone   almost everyone

some   none

From the kitchen of _____

Classroom Objects – Creativity Recipe Card 4

4A-Appetizer

Ingredients
Practice the classroom objects with the class. Have them repeat the words aloud with the entire class. Have them go online and search and print or write their list of classroom objects in your world language.

ACTFL: Presentational, Novice Low; **CEFR:** A1

How to do
Allow students to use YouTube and search for a list of TL classroom objects. Have them work in teams of four and ask a captain of each group to present the YouTube video to her/his/their team.

Time to do
20 minutes
Serves 4 to 32 students

Results
Who liked this appetizer? (Circle the response to this recipe.)

Everyone   almost everyone

some   none

From the kitchen of _____

Copyright material from Deborah Blaz and Tom Alsop (2023), *Sparking Creativity in the World Language Classroom: Strategies and Ideas to Build Your Students' Language Skills,* Routledge.

4B-Main Course

Ingredients
Use the list of classroom expressions that students made with the Appetizer card. Have a prize for the winning trio of students. The prize could be a star, button, sticker, candy, etc.

How to do
Have students work in groups of three. One student takes the role of teacher while asking questions to the other two students in the group. She/he is to ask questions in her/his/their world language saying "What is this?" to the other two students in the group. While asking the question, the teacher of each group points to a classroom object that is visible to the eye. The other two students answer say "It is ___" in the world language. The teacher in each group is to ask and point to ten different classroom objects while questioning. If students already know the colors, she/he can also ask what color the object is.

ACTFL: Interpersonal, Novice Mid; **CEFR:** A1

Time to do
15 minutes
Serves 3 to 30 students

Results
Who liked this main course? (Circle the response to this recipe.)

Everyone   almost everyone

some   none

From the kitchen of _____

Copyright material from Deborah Blaz and Tom Alsop (2023), *Sparking Creativity in the World Language Classroom: Strategies and Ideas to Build Your Students' Language Skills,* Routledge.

4C-Dessert

Ingredients
Use the list of words (classroom objects) from the Appetizer card. Have a prize for the winning team of students. Prize could be a star, button, sticker, candy, etc.

ACTFL: Presentational, Novice Low; **CEFR:** A1

How to do
Divide the class into two teams. Have each team select a classroom object as name in the TL for its team. Prepare a list of classroom object words – maybe ten to 15 classroom objects. Cut the words so that you can take one word and fold it up to hand to a student. Tell the students you are going to play Win-Lose-or-Draw. Appoint a scorekeeper. Have one student for each team be the drawer. Pick a good drawer. Have five words for each team. Take turns. Award one point for each word given that is correct. One student draws on the white board and the rest of the team of students guesses what the word for the object is in the TL.

Time to do
20 Minutes
Serves 1 to 30 students

Results
Who liked this dessert? (Circle the class response to this recipe.)

Everyone   almost everyone

some   none

From the kitchen of _____

Food (to like) – Creativity Recipe Card 5

5A-Appetizer

Ingredients
Review a list of "food vocabulary" aloud with the class. These words can come from your textbook or from an online list of foods found after searching the Internet. If you wish, let the students find the TL words for foods online via a search. Be sure to explain on the white board or smart board how to say "do you like" and "I like" or "I do not like" in their world language. For a bigger impact, bring in food from home (maybe in a grocery bag) to practice the words.

How to do
Have students work in groups of three. Assign one student in each group to be the captain of the group. They are to say aloud the "food words" in their TL. Explain to the students how to say "do you like" and "I like" in their world language. They each ask two questions to the other students in the group using "do you like" and then include a food. The other student responds, yes, or no, "I like" (or do not like) the food.

ACTFL: Presentational, Novice Mid; **CEFR:** A1

Time to do
15 minutes
Serves 3 to 30 students

Results
Who liked this appetizer? (Circle the response to this recipe.)

Everyone   almost everyone

some   none

From the kitchen of _____

Copyright material from Deborah Blaz and Tom Alsop (2023), *Sparking Creativity in the World Language Classroom: Strategies and Ideas to Build Your Students' Language Skills,* Routledge.

5B-Main Course

ACTFL: Presentational, Novice Low; **CEFR:** A1

Ingredients
Use the list of food words used from the Appetizer card. Ask students to prepare a food poster with the foods and then a short TV cooking show in Spanish. Students can use the poster with foods they have in their recipe. Students are to work in groups of three.

ACTFL: Presentational, Novice High; **CEFR:** A2

How to do
Students work in groups of three. Each one is to use their food poster to show the foods they are using in their appetizer, main course, or dessert. Two groups of three are to take turns presenting their TV cooking shows to the other group. Award a prize to the best trio of presenters. You can have groups present aloud at the same time. There will be lots of good noise while students are actively using their world language. Have students wear chef's hats!

Time to do
20 minutes
Serves 3 to 30 students

Results
Who liked this main course? (Circle the response to this recipe.)

Everyone   almost everyone

some   none

From the kitchen of _____

Copyright material from Deborah Blaz and Tom Alsop (2023), *Sparking Creativity in the World Language Classroom: Strategies and Ideas to Build Your Students' Language Skills*, Routledge.

5C-Dessert

Ingredients
Bring in some foods from home. Use food in bags, cartons, or cans. Write on the white board or onto the screen a name for your grocery store.

How to do
Divide the class into two teams. Have each team pick a name (using a TL word) for their team. Have one student keep score. Award one point for the student who raises her/his/their hand first after you take the food item out of the bag. Award a second point to the student if she/he/they can say "I like" and then name the food while speaking entirely in the TL. Award a food sticker to the best team!

ACTFL: Presentational, Novice Mid; **CEFR:** A1

Time to do
20 minutes
Serves 1 to 30 students

Results
Who liked this dessert? (Circle the class response to this recipe.)

Everyone   almost everyone

some   none

From the kitchen of _____

Copyright material from Deborah Blaz and Tom Alsop (2023), *Sparking Creativity in the World Language Classroom: Strategies and Ideas to Build Your Students' Language Skills,* Routledge.

Clothing – Creativity Recipe Card 6

6A-Appetizer

Ingredients

Pack your suitcase with 25 articles of clothing. Bring your suitcase to class. Ahead of time, prepare a handout with the 25 clothing words in your world language of the items in your suitcase. You could also put the list on a screen and not use a handout. Tell the class in your world language that you are going on a trip. Pull out an item of clothing and say in your world language you "have" that item of clothing.

ACTFL: Presentational, Novice Low; **CEFR:** A1

How to do

Students are to work in a group of four and draw or design an online ad for three items of clothing. They are to label all in their world language. Have one group present to another group in their teams of four. Award a prize to the best designer!

Time to do
20 minutes
Serves 4 to 30 students

Results
Who liked this appetizer? (Circle the response to this recipe.)

Everyone   almost everyone

some   none

From the kitchen of _____

Copyright material from Deborah Blaz and Tom Alsop (2023), *Sparking Creativity in the World Language Classroom: Strategies and Ideas to Build Your Students' Language Skills*, Routledge.

6B-Main Course

Ingredients
Use the list of "articles of clothing" that you used from the Appetizer card. Students are to plan a fashion show in their world language. Students are to work in groups of four.

How to do
Students are to plan the fashion show. One student in the group of four is to narrate in her/his/their world language what each of the other three is wearing.

ACTFL: Presentational, Novice High; **CEFR:** A2

Students who are modeling are to walk down a makeshift runway. Have students who are narrating say "I like" the dress, shoes, etc.

The narrator for each group can also say "(Name of student) is wearing" in her/his/their world language. Award an Oscar for the best fashion show. Props are fine! Wear sunglasses, lavish jewelry, earrings, nose rings, lip rings, etc. Incorporate the colors of the clothing in the description when possible. Have students take turns being the announcer.

Time to do
25 minutes
Serves 4 to 30 students

Results
Who liked this main course? (Circle your response to this recipe.)

Everyone   almost everyone

some   none

From the kitchen of _____

Copyright material from Deborah Blaz and Tom Alsop (2023), *Sparking Creativity in the World Language Classroom: Strategies and Ideas to Build Your Students' Language Skills*, Routledge.

6C-Dessert

Ingredients
Students are to use their list of clothing vocabulary from the Appetizer card. You need to prepare eight clothing words. Write out the words onto paper and cut each word up to use during the Win-Lose-or-Draw game.

> **ACTFL:** Interpretive, Novice Low; **CEFR:** A1

How to do
Play Win-Lose-or-Draw. Divide the class into two teams. Each team is to have a world language team name. Take turns. Appoint one student to keep score. Give a "No Homework Assignment" award to the winning team. Appoint two talented student drawers from each team to go the front of room. Hand one drawer from one team two articles of clothing to draw. Her/his/their team is to guess what the two items are. They have one minute to guess the two articles of clothing. The drawer for the second team is up next. She/he/they is to draw two articles of clothing and her/his/their team has one minute to guess the two articles of clothing in their world language. Have two rounds with each team taking one turn in each of the two rounds. In the event of a tie, both teams win the "No Homework Assignment" award!

Time to do
10 minutes
Serves 2 to 30 students

Results
Who liked this dessert? (Circle the class response to this recipe.)

Everyone   almost everyone

some   none

From the kitchen of _____

Copyright material from Deborah Blaz and Tom Alsop (2023), *Sparking Creativity in the World Language Classroom: Strategies and Ideas to Build Your Students' Language Skills,* Routledge.

Present Tense Verbs – Creativity Recipe Card 7

7A-Appetizer

Ingredients
Prepare a verb conjugation for a present tense regular verb. Use a chart you find online. Be sure the correct subject pronouns are listed with each verb ending.

How to do
Make a copy and hand out to your students or project the chart onto a screen. Have students repeat the correct subject pronoun with each correct verb form. Explain how this verb conjugation works in your world language. Review practical steps on how to conjugate the verb and what an infinitive is. Explain how the verb ending is dependent on the subject pronouns used. Break the class into pairs. Have students in the pairs take a turn conjugating the verb aloud.

ACTFL: Presentational, Novice Low; **CEFR:** A1

Time to do
15 minutes
Serves 2 to 30 students

Results
Who liked this appetizer? (Circle the response to this recipe.)

Everyone   almost everyone

some   none

From the kitchen of _____

Copyright material from Deborah Blaz and Tom Alsop (2023), *Sparking Creativity in the World Language Classroom: Strategies and Ideas to Build Your Students' Language Skills*, Routledge.

7B-Main Course

Ingredients
Review the verb conjugation and subject pronouns used on the Appetizer card. Prepare a Tic-Tac-Toe grid that includes in each box an infinitive with a subject pronoun. Be sure the infinitives pertain to the same conjugation as used on the Appetizer card - for example an -AR verb, or -ER verb or -IR verb in Spanish. Award a sticker, button, or fake money to the winning student in each trio.

> **ACTFL:** Presentational, Novice Low; **CEFR:** A1

How to do
Students can work in groups of three. Project the grid onto a screen or hand out copies of the grid. Have students use subject pronoun information from the Appetizer card. One student competes against another and the third student (the captain) marks the Xs and Os onto the grids as the students give the correct answer. The captain is to tell the student if she/he is correct. If so, the captain marks the grid with the X or O. The captain can draw the Tic-Tac-Toe grid on a piece of paper before starting the game should you not want to hand out the grid.

Time to do
20 minutes
Serves 3 to 30 students

Results
Who liked this main course? (Circle the response to this recipe.)

Everyone   almost everyone

some   none

From the kitchen of _____

Copyright material from Deborah Blaz and Tom Alsop (2023), *Sparking Creativity in the World Language Classroom: Strategies and Ideas to Build Your Students' Language Skills*, Routledge.

7C-Dessert

Ingredients
Prepare nine sentences that include subject pronouns and infinitives for three -AR, -ER, -IR verbs in Spanish or three equivalent verbs in your language. You may wish to use verbs similar to those used on the Appetizer card.

How to do
Cut the sentences into nine pieces - one for each sentence. Divide the class into two teams. Play Charades. One person from each team acts out the sentence given on the piece of paper while the rest of her/his/their team guesses the sentence in her/his/their world language. Take turns alternating between teams. Appoint a student to keep score. Allow each team up to two minutes to guess the sentence. Use different verbs/infinitives in the present tense. Each correct answer is worth five points. Award a prize to the winning team – extra credit points on the next quiz or test!

ACTFL: Presentational, Novice High; **CEFR:** A2

Time to do
20 minutes
Serves 2 to 30 students

Results
Who liked this dessert? (Circle the response to this recipe.)

Everyone   almost everyone

some   none

From the kitchen of _____

Copyright material from Deborah Blaz and Tom Alsop (2023), *Sparking Creativity in the World Language Classroom: Strategies and Ideas to Build Your Students' Language Skills,* Routledge.

Verb "to have" – Creativity Recipe Card 8

8A-Appetizer

Ingredients
Students learn how to conjugate the verb "to have" in the TL. Students are to work on YouTube using their tablets.

ACTFL: Presentational, Novice Low; **CEFR:** A1

How to do
Students are to work in pairs on their tablets. They are to find a YouTube video clip that explains how to conjugate the irregular verb "to have" in their TL. Students watch and listen to the conjugation and then take turns trying to conjugate the verb "to have." Students are to include the subject pronouns in their conjugations.

Time to do
15 minutes
Serves 2 to 30 students

Results
Who liked this appetizer? (Circle the response to this recipe.)

Everyone   almost everyone

some   none

From the kitchen of _____

Copyright material from Deborah Blaz and Tom Alsop (2023), *Sparking Creativity in the World Language Classroom: Strategies and Ideas to Build Your Students' Language Skills*, Routledge.

8B-Main Course

Ingredients
Use the YouTube video clip on how to conjugate "to have" from the Appetizer card. Have a prize for the winning group of students.

How to do
Divide the class into four groups. Students are to practice conjugating in the TL verb "to have" using the YouTube video clip that they used while working with the Appetizer card. Next, the students prepare a rap of the verb. Write a short script to use. Award two free nights of homework to the winning team. Teachers are to judge the presentations. Each group takes turns presenting their raps!

ACTFL: Presentational, Novice High; **CEFR:** A2+

Time to do
30 minutes – allow 15 minutes to prepare and 15 minutes to present.
Serves 4 to 30 students

Results
Who liked this main course? (Circle the response to this recipe.)

Everyone   almost everyone

some   none

From the kitchen of _____

8C-Dessert

Ingredients
Use the "to have" conjugation from the YouTube video clip used on the Appetizer card. Use world language expression stickers or flags for prizes.

ACTFL: Interpersonal, Novice Mid; **CEFR:** A2

How to do
Divide the class into four teams. Play an Ask Me a Question Game! Students are to ask you (teacher) questions in your world language using the verb "to have." You are to answer their questions as quickly as possible. The team asking you the most questions is the winner. Students can use interrogative words in their questions or ask without interrogative words. Appoint a student to keep score. Award stickers to the winning team.

Time to do
15 minutes
Serves 3 to 30 students

Results
Who liked this dessert? (Circle the response to this recipe.)

Everyone   almost everyone

some   none

From the kitchen of _____

Christmas Carols – Creativity Recipe Card 9

9A-Appetizer

Ingredients
You will need the lyrics to two Christmas carols in your TL. Get some TL bookmarks!

How to do
Divide the class into groups of five. Have a captain for each group. Hand out the lyrics to two TL Christmas carols. You may also use lyrics found online and project them onto the screen. Let students practice saying the words aloud and then sing the carols. Award a world language bookmark to the best group.

ACTFL: Presentational, Novice Mid; **CEFR:** A1

Time to do
25 minutes
Serves 5 to 30 students

Results
Who liked this appetizer? (Circle the response to this recipe.)

Everyone   almost everyone

some   none

From the kitchen of _____

Copyright material from Deborah Blaz and Tom Alsop (2023), *Sparking Creativity in the World Language Classroom: Strategies and Ideas to Build Your Students' Language Skills,* Routledge.

9B-Main Course

Ingredients
Use the lyrics to the same two Christmas carols on the Appetizer card. Get some world language pencils!

ACTFL: Presentational, Novice Mid; **CEFR:** A2

How to do
Students work in the same group of five formed for the Appetizer card. Practice the two Christmas carols aloud in your TL. Next, take your class to another world language class and sing your Christmas carols to them. For added fun, sing the two Christmas carols for your school administrators, choral department, athletic department, cafeteria workers, maintenance workers, etc. Video and show to classes. If possible, post the video on the school website. Award a world language pencil to the best group.

Time to do
30 minutes
Serves 5 to 30 students

Results
Who liked this main course? (Circle the response to this recipe.)

Everyone   almost everyone

some   none

From the kitchen of _____

Copyright material from Deborah Blaz and Tom Alsop (2023), *Sparking Creativity in the World Language Classroom: Strategies and Ideas to Build Your Students' Language Skills*, Routledge.

9C-Dessert

Ingredients
Use the lyrics for the same two Christmas carols found on the Appetizer card. Get some world language ball-point pens! Prepare a map that locates the homes you will visit to sing the two Christmas carols in your world language.

How to do
Students work in the same group of five used for the Appetizer card. Practice the two Christmas carols aloud in your world language. Select five to seven homes to visit. They can be teachers, administrators, patients in a hospital, homeless shelters, senior citizen residences, etc. Video your night of caroling and show to classes. If possible, put the video onto the school website. Award world language Christmas stickers to all participants.

ACTFL: Presentational, Novice Mid; **CEFR:** A2

Time to do
60–90 minutes; do this activity in the evening.
Serves 5 to 30 students

Results
Who liked this dessert? (Circle the response to this recipe.)

Everyone   almost everyone

some   none

From the kitchen of _____

Copyright material from Deborah Blaz and Tom Alsop (2023), *Sparking Creativity in the World Language Classroom: Strategies and Ideas to Build Your Students' Language Skills*, Routledge.

TL Music – Creativity Recipe Card 10

10A-Appetizer

Ingredients

Stream your favorite song in your TL. Make sure the singer is a favorite in your world language country! If possible, stream a video of the song and world language artist. Get some world language stickers to use for prizes.

ACTFL: Presentational, Novice Mid; **CEFR:** A2

How to do

Hand out the lyrics to the song or project them onto the screen. Have teams of six students practice the lyrics aloud in their group. If students have Internet access, let them find the appropriate website and practice. Have each group repeat the lyrics aloud in turns. Award world language stickers to the group with the most enthusiasm!

Time to do
20 minutes
Serves 6 to 30 students

Results

Who liked this appetizer? (Circle the response to this recipe.)

Everyone   almost everyone

some   none

From the kitchen of _____

Copyright material from Deborah Blaz and Tom Alsop (2023), *Sparking Creativity in the World Language Classroom: Strategies and Ideas to Build Your Students' Language Skills,* Routledge.

10B-Main Course

Ingredients
Use the lyrics to your favorite song in your world language from the Appetizer card. Use small pieces of candy for prizes.

How to do
Have students work in the same team of six as the one they were in for the Appetizer card. Students are to watch and listen to the video of the song by your favorite world language artist on their phones, laptops, or tablets. Have them practice singing the song aloud using a paper or electronic device with the lyrics. Remind them the day before to dress the part and bring props. Wear hats, sunglasses, jewelry, wigs, mustaches, beards, etc. Each group is to present/sing the song in front of the class. Award candy to the top two groups. Video the presentations and HAVE FUN!

ACTFL: Presentational, Novice Mid; **CEFR:** A2

Time to do
20 minutes
Serves 6 to 30 students

Results
Who liked this main course? (Circle the response to this recipe.)

Everyone   almost everyone

some   none

From the kitchen of _____

10C-Dessert

Ingredients
Use the lyrics to your favorite song in your world language from the Appetizer card. Award flag stickers to the best group.

ACTFL: Presentational, Novice Mid; **CEFR:** A2

How to do
Use the lyrics to your favorite song in your world language from the Appetizer card. Award flag stickers to the best group. This time, students are to lip-sync the song along with the video/song that they are watching on their electronic device. Make it funny! HAVE FUN! Video the presentations.

Time to do
20 minutes
Serves 6 to 30 students

Results
Who liked this dessert? (Circle the response to this recipe.)

Everyone   almost everyone

some   none

From the kitchen of _____

Copyright material from Deborah Blaz and Tom Alsop (2023), *Sparking Creativity in the World Language Classroom: Strategies and Ideas to Build Your Students' Language Skills,* Routledge.

LEVEL 2 – RECIPES 11–16

Vocabulary: Recipes 11–12
Grammar: Recipes 13–14
Culture: Recipes 15–16

Shopping Spree – Creativity Recipe Card 11

11A-Appetizer

Ingredients
Students do an online search to find words in their world language for items on their holiday shopping list. List the items by categories: clothes, toys, sports equipment, video games, games, jewelry, candy, TV, iPad, etc. Students can include at least one item for each category.

ACTFL: Interpretive, Novice Mid; **CEFR:** A1

How to do
Students are to work in pairs and read their shopping lists to the other student in their pair. Have students work together and compose a sentence in their world language for each of six shopping items on their list.

ACTFL: Presentational, Novice High; **CEFR:** A2

Time to do
20 minutes
Serves 2 to 30 students

Results
Who liked this appetizer? (Circle the response to this recipe.)

Everyone   almost everyone

some   none

From the kitchen of _____

Copyright material from Deborah Blaz and Tom Alsop (2023), *Sparking Creativity in the World Language Classroom: Strategies and Ideas to Build Your Students' Language Skills*, Routledge.

11B-Main Course

Ingredients
Students are to use their shopping list from the Appetizer card. Award candy to the winning pairs.

ACTFL: Presentational, Intermediate Mid;
CEFR: B1

How to do
Students are to work in groups of three. They are to prepare a script for a short skit in their world language where they go on a shopping spree. They create a problem they have when speaking with a clerk and solve that problem in their world language. Have them use their Google Translator to find vocabulary they may need in their skit. Have them practice the skits in their groups of three. Ask for volunteer groups to present in front of the class.

Time to do
25 minutes
Serves 3 to 30 students

Results
Who liked this main course? (Circle the response to this recipe.)

Everyone   almost everyone

some   none

From the kitchen of _____

11C-Dessert

Ingredients
Prepare a list of items you included on your holiday shopping list.

How to do
Divide the class into three teams. Have a student keep score. Read a sentence aloud in your world language where you describe in the world language ten items you are going to buy on your shopping spree. For example, describe what article of clothing you are buying without saying the word for the clothing. Do the same for a television, iPad, jewelry, sports equipment, toys, etc. Call on each team in turns or call on the first student to raise her/his/their hand after you say your sentence. The other team tries to guess the word that is being described.

ACTFL: Presentational, Intermediate Mid;
CEFR: B1

Time to do
10 minutes
Serves 3 to 30 students

Results
Who liked this dessert? (Circle the response to this recipe.)

Everyone   almost everyone

some   none

From the kitchen of _____

Copyright material from Deborah Blaz and Tom Alsop (2023), *Sparking Creativity in the World Language Classroom: Strategies and Ideas to Build Your Students' Language Skills*, Routledge.

Zoo – Creativity Recipe Card 12

12A-Appetizer

> **ACTFL:** Presentational, Novice High; **CEFR:** A2

Ingredients
Students go online to find a list of animal words. The animals should be animals who live in the zoo. They should find at least 12 animal words.

> **ACTFL:** Presentational, Novice High; **CEFR:** A2

How to do
Students are to work in pairs. Have them repeat aloud the words for the animals in their zoo. They are to compose aloud a sentence in their world language to describe each animal on their list of animals found in their zoo.

Time to do
15 minutes
Serves 2 to 30 students

Results
Who liked this appetizer? (Circle the response to this recipe.)

Everyone   almost everyone

some   none

From the kitchen of _____

Copyright material from Deborah Blaz and Tom Alsop (2023), *Sparking Creativity in the World Language Classroom: Strategies and Ideas to Build Your Students' Language Skills,* Routledge.

12B-Main Course

Ingredients
Students are to use the animal vocabulary from their list made from their work with the Appetizer card.

How to do
Students are to work in pairs. They are to prepare a dialogue of ten lines for two people who are on a visit to the zoo. One student is the parent and the other is the child. The parent describes each of the ten animals to the child while moving from cage to cage. At the end, create a problem that happens and solve it in your world language. For added fun, let the child describe the animals to the parent.

ACTFL: Presentational, Intermediate Mid;
CEFR: B1+

Time to do
25 minutes
Serves 2 to 30 students

Results
Who liked this main course? (Circle the response to this recipe.)

Everyone   almost everyone

some   none

From the kitchen of _____

12C-Dessert

Ingredients
Scramble the names of 15 animals in your world language. Get some animal stickers in your TL, or animal crackers, for prizes.

ACTFL: Presentational, Novice High; **CEFR:** A2

How to do
Divide the class into three teams. Project the scrambled words onto a screen. Appoint a student to keep score. Award one point for the student who unscrambles the word in her/his/their world language. Award a second point to the student who can compose a sentence aloud in her/his/their world language using the unscrambled word in the sentence. Award animal stickers for prizes. You may also award animal crackers for prizes.

Time to do
15 minutes
Serves 2 to 30 students

Results
Who liked this dessert? (Circle the response to this recipe.)

Everyone   almost everyone

some   none

From the kitchen of _____

Copyright material from Deborah Blaz and Tom Alsop (2023), *Sparking Creativity in the World Language Classroom: Strategies and Ideas to Build Your Students' Language Skills*, Routledge.

Past Tense(s) – Creativity Recipe Card 13

13A-Appetizer

Ingredients
Consult the section in your textbook for conjugating and understanding verbs in one or two past tenses in the indicative mood of your world language. Students work alone and review these pages.

ACTFL: Presentational, Intermediate Mid;
CEFR: B1

Have students make and design a one-page entry for a student journal. Students are to write an entry in their world language of eight to ten sentences using one or two past tenses in their world language.

How to do
Have students make and design a one-page entry for their student journal. Students are to write an entry in their world language of eight to ten sentences using one or two past tenses in their world language as they write about what she/he did yesterday and last night.

ACTFL: Presentational, Intermediate Mid;
CEFR: B1

Time to do
20 minutes
Serves 1 to 30 students

Results
Who liked this appetizer? (Circle the response to this recipe.)

Everyone   almost everyone

some   none

From the kitchen of _____

Copyright material from Deborah Blaz and Tom Alsop (2023), *Sparking Creativity in the World Language Classroom: Strategies and Ideas to Build Your Students' Language Skills,* Routledge.

13B-Main Course

Ingredients
Consult the section in your textbook for conjugating and understanding verbs in one or two past tenses in the indicative mood of your world language. Have students review these pages in pairs.

ACTFL: Presentational, Intermediate Mid;
CEFR: B1+

How to do
Students are to work in pairs. They are to prepare a short news report in their world language on what both of them did yesterday. Students are to make things funny. The sentences need not be true. Ask students to volunteer to present their news show on TV in front of the class. Video the presentations. Award extra credit points to the best presenters!

Time to do
20 minutes
Serves 2 to 30 students

Results
Who liked this main course? (Circle the response to this recipe.)

Everyone   almost everyone

some   none

From the kitchen of _____

Copyright material from Deborah Blaz and Tom Alsop (2023), *Sparking Creativity in the World Language Classroom: Strategies and Ideas to Build Your Students' Language Skills,* Routledge.

13C-Dessert

Ingredients
Have students review one or two past tenses in their world language using their textbooks or a review sheet handout. You (teacher) are to make up ten questions in the past tense and ask those questions to each team.

How to do
Play "Answer the Question" game. Divide the class into two teams. Have teams take turns answering the questions in their world language. Have a student keep score. Award candy to the team that answers the most questions. For added fun, have students ask a question in their world language using a verb in the past tense in their questions. Try to use interrogative words!

ACTFL: Interpersonal/Presentational, Intermediate Mid;
CEFR: B1

Time to do
15 minutes
Serves 2 to 30 students

Results
Who liked this dessert? (Circle the response to this recipe.)

Everyone   almost everyone

some   none

From the kitchen of _____

Commands – Creativity Recipe Card 14

14A-Appetizer

Ingredients
Have students review how to give commands in their world language. Use their textbooks or hand out a worksheet on commands.

ACTFL: Interpersonal, Intermediate Low;
CEFR: A2

How to do
Students are to work in pairs. Have them take turns giving each other a command in their world language. Have each student give three commands. The other student is to act out the command!

Time to do
15 minutes
Serves 2 to 30 students

Results
Who liked this appetizer? (Circle the response to this recipe.)

Everyone   almost everyone

some   none

From the kitchen of _____

Copyright material from Deborah Blaz and Tom Alsop (2023), *Sparking Creativity in the World Language Classroom: Strategies and Ideas to Build Your Students' Language Skills,* Routledge.

14B-Main Course

Ingredients
Make up a list of practical commands to give a small group in which the instructor in each group gives commands in her/his/their language to the others in the group. They are to do the command in an exercise class.

How to do
Have students work in groups of four as they review how to give commands in their world language. One student in each group is the group instructor at a gym class and she/he gives commands in her/his/their world language using these verbs: work, jump, run, stop, start, lift, turn off/on the light, stand on one foot, walk fast, rest, etc. Pick three commands for each group. Award a prize to the best exercise class. Make this activity a "no homework night."

ACTFL: Presentational (instructor) Interpretive (listener), Novice High; **CEFR:** A2

Time to do
20 minutes
Serves 4 to 30 students

Results
Who liked this main course? (Circle the response to this recipe.)

Everyone   almost everyone

some   none

From the kitchen of _____

Copyright material from Deborah Blaz and Tom Alsop (2023), *Sparking Creativity in the World Language Classroom: Strategies and Ideas to Build Your Students' Language Skills*, Routledge.

14C-Dessert

Ingredients
Prepare 15 verbs in the command form for use in the game Charades.

ACTFL: Interpretive, Novice Mid; **CEFR:** A1

How to do
Divide the class into two teams. Appoint a student to keep score. Have students act out a verb that is a command such as walk, run, sleep, eat, listen, speak, etc. Each team is to act out seven verbs. Let students volunteer to act out the command.

Time to do
20 minutes
Serves 2 to 30 students

Results
Who liked this dessert? (Circle the response to this recipe.)

Everyone   almost everyone

some   none

From the kitchen of _____

Dance – Creativity Recipe Card 15

15A-Appetizer

Ingredients
Students are to do an online search and learn basic steps for a dance that is native to one of their world language countries.

ACTFL: Interpretive, Novice Mid; **CEFR:** A1

How to do
Students work in pairs. They are to use their online dance information to study the various steps of the dance. They are to use YouTube to view a video of the chosen dance.

ACTFL: Interpretive, Novice Mid; **CEFR:** A1

Time to do
15 minutes
Serves 2 to 30 students

Results
Who liked this appetizer? (Circle the response to this recipe.)

Everyone   almost everyone

some   none

From the kitchen of _____

15B-Main Course

Ingredients
Students use information from their online search and YouTube video about the dance they chose.

> **ACTFL:** Presentational, Intermediate Mid;
> **CEFR:** B1

How to do
Students work in pairs. They practice the dance and then present the dance to the entire class. The class stands up and follows the pair who gives instructions in their world language on HOW TO DO the steps. The pair also projects the YouTube video clip so the class can view the dance steps. Ask pairs to volunteer to present and teach their dance to the class. Award stickers or candy to the best presenters and dancers!

Time to do
25 minutes
Serves 2 to 30 students

Results
Who liked this main course? (Circle the response to this recipe.)

Everyone   almost everyone

some   none

From the kitchen of _____

15C-Dessert

Ingredients
Students use information from their online search and YouTube video.

How to do
Students work in pairs. Have a drawing contest. Students are to draw a picture of one or two dancers doing the dance chosen by the pair. They are to label the dance and any words to describe the drawing in their world language. Give an "Artist of the Day" award for the best original drawings.

Time to do
15 minutes
Serves 2 to 30 students

Results
Who liked this dessert? (Circle the response to this recipe.)

Everyone   almost everyone

some   none

From the kitchen of _____

Copyright material from Deborah Blaz and Tom Alsop (2023), *Sparking Creativity in the World Language Classroom: Strategies and Ideas to Build Your Students' Language Skills,* Routledge.

Celebrities – Creativity Recipe Card 16

16A-Appetizer

Ingredients
Students go online and gather information on a famous celebrity from their TL country. The celebrity should be a movie star, a singer, or athlete. Each student is to gather information on a different celebrity.

ACTFL: Interpersonal, Novice Mid; **CEFR:** A1

How to do
Students work in pairs. They are to share their online information with the other student in the pair. Each student is to take notes and list key information about their celebrity.

Time to do
20 minutes
Serves 2 to 30 students

Results
Who liked this appetizer? (Circle the response to this recipe.)

Everyone   almost everyone

some   none

From the kitchen of _____

Copyright material from Deborah Blaz and Tom Alsop (2023), *Sparking Creativity in the World Language Classroom: Strategies and Ideas to Build Your Students' Language Skills*, Routledge.

16B-Main Course

Ingredients
Students use the information from their online exploration of their celebrity.

How to do
Students work in pairs. They are to dress up like the celebrity and write a short dialogue between the two celebrities. They are to role-play the two celebrities who meet by chance in a famous world city. Students volunteer to act out their role-plays. Give a "Best Dressed" award and "Best Actor/Actress" award to the best pairs!

ACTFL: Interpretive, Intermediate Mid;
CEFR: B1

Time to do
20 minutes
Serves 2 to 30 students

Results
Who liked this main course? (Circle the response to this recipe.)

Everyone   almost everyone

some   none

From the kitchen of _____

Copyright material from Deborah Blaz and Tom Alsop (2023), *Sparking Creativity in the World Language Classroom: Strategies and Ideas to Build Your Students' Language Skills*, Routledge.

16C-Dessert

Ingredients
You (teacher) prepare a list of three celebrities from your world-language country. Write sentences for each celebrity that include what they do, where they live, and why they are famous.

ACTFL: Interpretive, Novice High; **CEFR:** A2

How to do
Hand out the list that you prepared for the ten celebrities. Students are to refer to your list while playing "Celebrity Bowl." Divide the class into two teams. Have a student keep score. Award extra credit points for class participation to the winning team. You are to ask two questions in your world language for each of the three celebrities. Students are to answer in their world language.

Time to do
15 minutes
Serves 2 to 30 students

Results
Who liked this dessert? (Circle the response to this recipe.)

Everyone   almost everyone

some   none

From the kitchen of _____

ADVANCED LEVELS – RECIPES 17–22

Vocabulary: Recipes 17–18
Grammar: Recipes 19–20
Culture: Recipe 21–22

Hospital – Creativity Recipe Card 17

17A-Appetizer

Ingredients
Students do an online search and find 20 words of hospital vocabulary in the TL such as "hospital words in Spanish," etc.

> **ACTFL:** Interpretive, Novice Mid; **CEFR:** A1

How to do
Students work in groups of four. They are to practice saying aloud their list of 20 hospital words. They then compose a sentence in Spanish using five of their words. Students are to take turns in the group of four.

> **ACTFL:** Presentational, Novice High; **CEFR:** A2

Time to do
15 minutes
Serves 4 to 30 students

Results
Who liked this appetizer? (Circle the response to this recipe.)

Everyone   almost everyone

some   none

From the kitchen of _____

Copyright material from Deborah Blaz and Tom Alsop (2023), *Sparking Creativity in the World Language Classroom: Strategies and Ideas to Build Your Students' Language Skills,* Routledge.

17B-Main Course

Ingredients
Students use their list of "hospital words" from the Appetizer Page.

> **ACTFL:** Presentational, Intermediate High;
> **CEFR:** B1+

How to do
Students use their hospital words in their group of four and include some of their words in a skit that takes place at the hospital. Each group gives their skit a title. Students write the skit. One student is the doctor, another is a nurse, one is a patient, and the final person is a friend of the patient. The injured student is the patient while her/his/their friend accompanies her into the ER at the hospital. There is a problem and students and medical personnel solve the problem. Skits can be fun and humorous! Dress the parts. Have props that include a sign with the name of the hospital. Students are to all work in their world language. Have each group present their skit in front of the class. Give a "Best Actor/Actress" award to the best group. Video the skits!

Time to do
15 minutes
Serves 4 to 30 students

Results
Who liked this main course? (Circle the response to this recipe.)

Everyone   almost everyone

some   none

From the kitchen of _____

Copyright material from Deborah Blaz and Tom Alsop (2023), *Sparking Creativity in the World Language Classroom: Strategies and Ideas to Build Your Students' Language Skills*, Routledge.

17C-Dessert

Ingredients
Use the students' hospital words lists.

How to do
You (teacher) are to compose 12 sentences in your world language. Divide the class into three groups. Give four sentences to each group to act out. Play "Hospital Charades." One student acts out the sentence for her/his/their group. Take turns alternating the groups. Sentences should each contain one or two hospital words. Have one student keep score. Students have two minutes to guess the sentence. Award two points for each correct answer. Give "The ER Acting" award to the best group!

ACTFL: Presentational, Intermediate Mid;
CEFR: A2+

Time to do
15 minutes
Serves 4 to 30 students

Results
Who liked this dessert? (Circle the response to this recipe.)

Everyone   almost everyone

some   none

From the kitchen of _____

Copyright material from Deborah Blaz and Tom Alsop (2023), *Sparking Creativity in the World Language Classroom: Strategies and Ideas to Build Your Students' Language Skills,* Routledge.

Hotel Vocab – Creativity Recipe Card 18

18A-Appetizer

> **ACTFL:** Interpretive, Novice Mid; **CEFR:** A1

> **ACTFL:** Presentational, Novice High; **CEFR:** A2

Ingredients
Students do an online search and find 20 words of hotel vocabulary in the TL such as "hotel words in (TL)," etc.

How to do
Students work in groups of three. They are to practice saying aloud their list of 20 hotel words. They then compose a sentence in the TL using four of their words. Students are to take turns in the group of three.

Time to do
15 minutes
Serves 3 to 30 students

Results
Who liked this appetizer? (Circle the response to this recipe.)

Everyone   almost everyone

some   none

From the kitchen of _____

Copyright material from Deborah Blaz and Tom Alsop (2023), *Sparking Creativity in the World Language Classroom: Strategies and Ideas to Build Your Students' Language Skills*, Routledge.

18B-Main Course

Ingredients
Use the students' hotel words lists.

How to do
Students use their hotel words in their group of three and include some of their words in a skit that takes place at the hotel. Each group gives their skit a title. Students write the skit. One student is the hotel worker, one is a student, and the final person is a friend of the student. There is a problem and students and the hotel worker solve the problem. Skits can be fun and humorous! Dress the parts. Have props that include a sign with the name of the hotel. Students are to do all work in their world language. Have each group present their skit in front of the class. Give a "Best Actor/Actress" award to the best group. Video the skits!

ACTFL: Presentational, Intermediate High; **CEFR:** B2

Time to do
15 minutes
Serves 3 to 30 students

Results
Who liked this main course? (Circle the response to this recipe.)

Everyone   almost everyone

some   none

From the kitchen of _____

Copyright material from Deborah Blaz and Tom Alsop (2023), *Sparking Creativity in the World Language Classroom: Strategies and Ideas to Build Your Students' Language Skills*, Routledge.

18C-Dessert

Ingredients
Write a list of the hotel words used by the students. Add some of your own. Write in your world language seven problems that a make-believe hotel is having.

ACTFL: Presentational, Intermediate Mid;
CEFR: B1

How to do
Play the game "Solve the Problem." Have three students in a group. Ask a student to be the scorekeeper. Award a point to each group for each solution that a student can give to each problem. You are to be the judge and decide whether to accept the student's solution. Award a free "Week in an Imaginary Hotel called the Problems Hotel" in your TL country. All speaking must be in the world language!

Time to do
15 minutes
Serves 3 to 30 students

Results
Who liked this dessert? (Circle the response to this recipe.)

Everyone   almost everyone

some   none

From the kitchen of _____

Copyright material from Deborah Blaz and Tom Alsop (2023), *Sparking Creativity in the World Language Classroom: Strategies and Ideas to Build Your Students' Language Skills*, Routledge.

Present Subjunctive – Creativity Recipe Card 19

19A-Appetizer

Ingredients
Use a chapter from the textbook, an online explanation, or your handouts, for the explanations and practice using the present subjunctive in your world language.

How to do
Students are to use their textbooks or your handouts to review the present subjunctive in their world language. They are to work in groups of four. Students are to take turns answering questions from their textbook or handouts using the present subjunctive. The captain of the group directs the questions to each member of the group. Have students repeat the sentences using the present subjunctive aloud in their groups.

ACTFL: Presentational, Novice High; **CEFR:** B1

Time to do
15 minutes
Serves 4 to 30 students

Results
Who liked this appetizer? (Circle the response to this recipe.)

Everyone   almost everyone

some   none

From the kitchen of _____

Copyright material from Deborah Blaz and Tom Alsop (2023), *Sparking Creativity in the World Language Classroom: Strategies and Ideas to Build Your Students' Language Skills,* Routledge.

19B-Main Course

Ingredients
Use explanations for the present subjunctive from work students did on the Appetizer card.

ACTFL: Presentational, Intermediate Mid;
CEFR: B1

How to do
Students write a script for an evening news show on a popular TV channel. Each group of four gives their skit a title. Each of the four students says a sentence in the present subjunctive from her/his/their script while giving the evening news. One student introduces the TV news show. Each skit can be fun and humorous! Dress the parts. Have props that include a sign with the name of the TV news program. Students are to do all work in their world language. Have each group present their skit/newscast in front of the class. Give a "Broadcast of the Year" award to the best group. Video the skits!

Time to do
25 minutes
Serves 4 to 30 students

Results
Who liked this main course? (Circle the response to this recipe.)

Everyone   almost everyone

some   none

From the kitchen of _____

Copyright material from Deborah Blaz and Tom Alsop (2023), *Sparking Creativity in the World Language Classroom: Strategies and Ideas to Build Your Students' Language Skills*, Routledge.

19C-Dessert

Ingredients
Use explanations for the present subjunctive from work they did on the Appetizer card.

How to do
You (teacher) are to compose 14 questions using the present subjunctive in your world language. Have each team take a turn. Give two questions to each group of four. Take turns alternating the groups. Award one point for each correct answer. If a student misses another team can give the correct answer and earn the point. The team with the most points is the winner of the "Present Subjunctive Expert Game."

ACTFL: Interpretive, Intermediate Mid;
CEFR: B1

Time to do
15 minutes
Serves 4 to 28 students

Results
Who liked this dessert? (Circle the response to this recipe.)

Everyone   almost everyone

some   none

From the kitchen of _____

Past Subjunctive – Creativity Recipe Card 20

20A-Appetizer

Ingredients
Use a chapter from the textbook, an online explanation, or your handouts for the explanations and practice using the past subjunctive in your world language.

ACTFL: Presentational, Intermediate Mid;
CEFR: B1

How to do
Students are to use their textbooks, information from an online search, or handouts to review the past subjunctive in their world language. They are to work in groups of four. Students are to take turns writing short world-language translations using the past subjunctive, which is English. The captain of the group directs the past subjunctive practice. Have students repeat the translations aloud in their world language.

Time to do
20 minutes
Serves 4 to 28 students

Results
Who liked this appetizer? (Circle the response to this recipe.)

Everyone   almost everyone

some   none

From the kitchen of _____

Copyright material from Deborah Blaz and Tom Alsop (2023), *Sparking Creativity in the World Language Classroom: Strategies and Ideas to Build Your Students' Language Skills*, Routledge.

20B-Main Course

Ingredients
Use explanations for the past subjunctive from work the students on the Appetizer card.

How to do
Students write an article for a popular online newspaper in their world language. Students are to work in pairs. The article needs to have four sentences using the past subjunctive. There should be a total of 20 lines in the article. The article can be about sports, or music, a singer, politician, movie star, etc. Students are to do all work in their world language. Have each group read their article aloud in front of the class. Give the article a catchy title! Give a "Writer of the Year" award to the best pair. Video the oral presentations!

> **ACTFL:** Presentational, Intermediate Mid;
> **CEFR:** B1+

Time to do
20 minutes
Serves 2 to 30 students

Results
Who liked this main course? (Circle the response to this recipe.)

Everyone   almost everyone

some   none

From the kitchen of _____

Copyright material from Deborah Blaz and Tom Alsop (2023), *Sparking Creativity in the World Language Classroom: Strategies and Ideas to Build Your Students' Language Skills*, Routledge.

20C-Dessert

Ingredients
Prepare ten sentences in English using the past subjunctive. Have lots of markers at the white board.

ACTFL: Interpretive, Intermediate Mid;
CEFR: B1+

How to do
Have a "White Board Race." Use the sentences you have prepared. Divide the class into three teams. Appoint one student to be scorekeeper. Read a sentence aloud to the class using the past subjunctive in each of the sentences. One student from each team is to race to the white board and write the translation to your sentence in the world language. The first student who finishes translating the sentence correctly gets the point for her/his/their team.

Time to do
15 minutes
Serves 2 to 30 students

Results
Who liked this dessert? (Circle the response to this recipe.)

Everyone   almost everyone

some   none

From the kitchen of _____

Copyright material from Deborah Blaz and Tom Alsop (2023), *Sparking Creativity in the World Language Classroom: Strategies and Ideas to Build Your Students' Language Skills,* Routledge.

Writer's Day – Creativity Recipe Card 21

21A-Appetizer

Ingredients
Give students a short story in their world language or a chapter from a short novel.

How to do
Hand out the short story or a chapter from a short novel. Students are to work in pairs and read and speak in their world language while summarizing and giving highlights in their world language about the content and meaning of the story or chapter they are reading. Have students list ten important vocabulary words in their reading. Use the same story for the entire class.

ACTFL: Presentational, Intermediate Mid;
CEFR: B2

Time to do
15 minutes
Serves 2 to 30 students

Results
Who liked this appetizer? (Circle the response to this recipe.)

Everyone   almost everyone

some   none

From the kitchen of _____

Copyright material from Deborah Blaz and Tom Alsop (2023), *Sparking Creativity in the World Language Classroom: Strategies and Ideas to Build Your Students' Language Skills,* Routledge.

21B-Main Course

Ingredients
Students use the same short story or chapter from a short novel as those from the Appetizer card.

> **ACTFL:** Presentational, Intermediate Mid;
> **CEFR:** B1

How to do
Students work in pairs. They are to write a one paragraph summary in their world language of the short story or chapter from a short novel. Have students read their summaries to the class. Award a free night of homework to the students who give the best summaries!

Time to do
20 minutes
Serves 2 to 30 students

Results
Who liked the main course? (Circle your response to this recipe.)

Everyone   almost everyone

some   none

From the kitchen of _____

Copyright material from Deborah Blaz and Tom Alsop (2023), *Sparking Creativity in the World Language Classroom: Strategies and Ideas to Build Your Students' Language Skills,* Routledge.

21C-Dessert

Ingredients
Give the students a topic for an imaginary short, short story, such as the dancing dog, the singing ants, a night in grammar land, the talking coffee cup, the magic car, etc.

How to do
Students work in pairs. They have three minutes to think of some sentences to include in the imaginary short, short story pertaining to the title you have provided from above (or your own title).

ACTFL: Presentational, Intermediate Mid;
CEFR: B1

Have students make up and say a sentence in their world language to help compose the short, short story. Award a point to each pair for sentences given for the short story. Have a student keep score. Have another student write down the sentences on a white board. Try to get ten to 15 sentences. Make up a fun beginning, middle, and end for the short, short story. Give the "Writer of the Day" award to the winning pair. Award extra points if the students use the subjunctive in the story.

Time to do
20 minutes
Serves 2 to 30 students

Results
Who liked this dessert? (Circle the response to this recipe.)

Everyone   almost everyone

some   none

From the kitchen of _____

Poetry – Creativity Recipe Card 22

22A-Appetizer

Ingredients

Prepare a handout with a well-known short poem by a famous poet in your world language. Include a short biography. Include a vocabulary list with difficult-to-understand words.

ACTFL: Presentational, Intermediate Mid;
CEFR: B1

How to do

Hand out the poem and biography. Students are to work in pairs. Read the short poem aloud with the class. Have each pair write a short summary in their world language of the meaning of the poem. Award some extra credit points to the pairs who read their summaries to the class.

Time to do
20 minutes
Serves 2 to 30 students

Results

Who liked this appetizer? (Circle the response to this recipe.)

Everyone   almost everyone

some   none

From the kitchen of _____

Copyright material from Deborah Blaz and Tom Alsop (2023), *Sparking Creativity in the World Language Classroom: Strategies and Ideas to Build Your Students' Language Skills*, Routledge.

22B-Main Course

Ingredients
Students are to use the handout of the short poem provided on the Appetizer card.

How to do
Have the students work in pairs. They are to practice reading the poem in their world language. Have a live poetry reading of the poem. Have students dress the part. They can wear sunglasses, "poetic" clothes, etc. Have pairs volunteer to do a reading of the TL poem in front of the class. Give "The Poetry Reader of the Day" award to the best pairs. Award as an extra prize, such as a free night from homework, to the pair who recite the poem from memory without looking at the paper!

ACTFL: Presentational, Intermediate Mid;
CEFR: B1

Time to do
15 minutes
Serves 2 to 30 students

Results
Who liked this main course? (Circle your response to this recipe.)

Everyone   almost everyone

some   none

From the kitchen of _____

Copyright material from Deborah Blaz and Tom Alsop (2023), *Sparking Creativity in the World Language Classroom: Strategies and Ideas to Build Your Students' Language Skills,* Routledge.

218 ♦ My Creativity Recipe Cards

22C-Dessert

Ingredients
Provide a handout with a list of possible titles for a short poem. You might include: "A beautiful person," "My special dog," "Long days," "You," "Unforgettable," "Wish…," "If I were…," "It was possible…," "I want…," "The moon," "The night," "Paris," "Madrid," "Frankfurt," "Rome," etc.

ACTFL: Presentational, Intermediate High; **CEFR:** B1+

How to do
Have the students work in pairs. They are to use some of the titles from the handout page or provide their own titles. Each pair is to write a short poem in their world language. Have them use the present subjunctive. Let the super grammarians use some "if " clauses! Poems should be eight to 12 lines in length. Have pairs read their poem aloud, in their world language, to the class. Give "The Poets of the Day" award to the pairs with the best poem and reading of their poem.

Time to do
20 minutes
Serves 2 to 30 students

Results
Who liked this dessert? (Circle your response to this recipe.)

Everyone   almost everyone

some   none

From the kitchen of _____

Copyright material from Deborah Blaz and Tom Alsop (2023), *Sparking Creativity in the World Language Classroom: Strategies and Ideas to Build Your Students' Language Skills,* Routledge.

My Own Recipes Created by ME

Please create and use your own Recipe Cards as well as those in this book!

Level   **Topic** _____

My Creativity Recipe

ACTFL Proficiency Level:

A – Appetizer

Ingredients

How to do

Time to do

Serves

Results
Who liked this appetizer? (Circle the response to this recipe.)

Everyone   almost everyone

some   none

From the kitchen of _____

Copyright material from Deborah Blaz and Tom Alsop (2023), *Sparking Creativity in the World Language Classroom: Strategies and Ideas to Build Your Students' Language Skills*, Routledge.

ACTFL Proficiency Level: _____

B – Main Course

Ingredients

How to do

Time to do

Serves

Results
Who liked the main course?
(Circle the response to this recipe.)

Everyone   almost everyone

some   none

From the kitchen of _____

ACTFL Proficiency Level: _____

C – Dessert

Ingredients

How to do

Time to do

Serves

Results
Who liked this dessert? (Circle the response to this recipe.)

Everyone   almost everyone

some   none

From the kitchen of _____

11

Stimulating Creativity in My Students

Introduction

This chapter focuses on methods to stimulate creativity in students: first, by modeling it yourself, but other strategies such as using curiosity, hooks, RAFT assignments for writing, chat mats for speaking, and choice boards for differentiated homework or virtual assignments. Tom has also contributed 24 low-prep and FUN creativity starter cards for an easy-to-use **creativity boost,** as well as a template for creating your own.

Modeling

Now it is time to focus on how to stimulate creativity in your students. You have modeled it well for them by using all the strategies in the first ten chapters. Now, harness students' curiosity with hooks, give them chat mats to enhance speaking, and RAFT assignments or choice boards for differentiated products that appeal to their unique talents, and which are MUCH more fun to evaluate since they will lack the cookie-cutter sameness of more structured specifications. Here are 24 low-prep and truly FUN creativity starters for an easy boost, and a template for creating your own inspirations.

The best stimulation for creativity is to model it, so you are on the right track in wanting to be more creative. Be the model by trying new activities, introducing new people and cultures to your students. Make your classroom a place of constant variety and change, with stability in expectations and classroom management, of course.

Ask questions and question answers with your students. Leading questions ("what if…") stimulate more creative responses.

Use hooks. There are none better for stimulating creativity than Dave Burgess's hooks in *Teach Like a Pirate* (see Sources) to get students excited about the lesson. Curiosity is a great stimulant for creativity, and again, you are modeling creativity from the very start of the lesson.

Strategies to Guarantee Creative Responses from Students

I think students' biggest stumbling block in getting creative is having the initial idea. If that is the case, all the questions in the beginning of Chapter 3 might be a good starting point for them. Or, you can choose the topic, and use one of the following to give them enough support to spread their creative wings.

RAFT

ACTFL: Presentational, Intermediate Mid and above; **CEFR:** B1

Using the acronym for Role, Audience, Form, and Topic, a RAFT is an assignment that gives students rather specific choices in the product they will produce. In a RAFT, you can give choices of writing or speaking from several viewpoints. Figure 11.1 is a typical RAFT for a unit on weather.

Figure 11.1 RAFT

This could be used at the ACTFL Novice level if output was a list of weather expressions, at the Intermediate Low level if in sentence form, and Intermediate High level if students are expected to show voice			
ROLE	**AUDIENCE**	**FORMAT**	**TOPIC**
Meteorologist	Family member	Email or text	Severe weather coming
Journalist	Local people	News article	Local destruction due to weather
Tree	Birds and squirrels that live in/on me	Speech	Cold weather on the way
Historian	Earth science students	Worksheet to fill in	Local weather trends
Or suggest your own!			

If you feel creatively challenged, use the online RAFT generator for inspiration: http://classroomcommons.blogspot.com/2013/11/historyfix-raft-writing-prompts-for.html

Placemats/Chat Mats

Even if you have not ditched your textbook for comprehensive input (CI) teaching as I have, a placemat is indispensable as support for conversations and writing. These are a one- or two-sided papers containing key words and phrases for the unit being studied, plus common exclamations, transitions, or grammar charts. With questions and answers right in front of them, students will quickly be able to converse or write in the TL. Amy Leonard has a wonderful set of free, highly recommended chat mats for Spanish, French, and German at *Amy's Chat Mats* (https://wakelet.com/wake/mJIOim9REP4WFyhLBi9KE). Bethanie Drew offers weekend chat maps in Spanish, French and German as well (https://aventurasnuevas.wordpress.com/2018/09/03/weekend-chat-update-structures-to-support-student-learning-and-teacher-sanity-part-4/).

> **ACTFL:** Interpersonal, Novice Mid and above; **CEFR:** A1

Choice Boards (Tic-Tac-Toe, sometimes called noughts and crosses)

A choice board gives students voice and choice in how they practice a topic or theme. It is a grid of three (or five) rows across and the same number of columns, which is why it is often called a Tic-Tac-Toe board. The grid is populated with a wide variety of assignments carefully placed so that in any one direction, there is a variety of tasks: speaking, reading, listening, and writing. It takes a while to create a good one, as you also need to consider the rigor of the activities in every possible direction. Figure 11.2 is a sample choice board for the beginning of the year Level 1 Novice students.

> **ACTFL:** All types, all levels; **CEFR:** all levels

There are a variety of ways to assign a choice board. You can tell students to do all the activities in a row horizontally, vertically, or diagonally (as in tic-tac-toe). You can also put the product you want everyone

Figure 11.2 Tic-tac-toe Greetings

ACTFL Novice Low level		
Greet five classmates, and write down who you greeted, and what they answered.	Read the story and write answers to the questions.	Sort the vocabulary phrases on Jamboard into matching pairs.
Do the EdPuzzle on greetings.	Make a cartoon about greeting a Spanish-speaking foreign exchange student.	With a classmate and both of you pretending to be someone famous, make a FlipGrid of you greeting each other.
Read the rebus story aloud to a classmate, replacing the pictures with the appropriate words.	Watch the video and write down two tips for a visiting American on how to properly greet someone in that country.	Identify the people on the list as tú or usted.

to do at the center and assign completion of all activities in a row in any direction that goes through the center square. You can assign the board and tell students to do any three (or four or five) squares that touch. Students will of course usually choose the one that sounds easiest or more fun, so the ones nearby need to enlarge the demands by assigning tasks that require students to perform in a way that is less in their comfort zones. I generally specify how many activities I require them to accomplish in a class period to keep them focused on the task at hand.

The idea(s) that I'd like students to try FIRST:_____

_____

What topic(s) can I use this for? _____

_____

Creativity Starter 1 – Crazy clothes

ACTFL: Interpersonal/presentational, Novice Mid; **CEFR:** A1

Teacher activity: Wear an outfit which is really zany in color and/or in appearance. Watch the students' reactions. Have them comment in the TL!

Student activity: Have students write a description of your clothes in the TL. Spin the description into a short, short story.

Creativity Starter 2 – Serenade a student

ACTFL: Presentational, Novice Mid; **CEFR:** A2

Teacher activity: Serenade a student in your class in your world language! Make the song be a traditional or popular one in your world language.

Students may comment in the TL.

Student activity: Have students practice in pairs and present/sing a song in the TL. Let a few students serenade a few other students.

Creativity Starter 3 – Silence, please

ACTFL: Presentational, Intermediate Mid; **CEFR:** B1

Teacher activity: Enter your room and say nothing for the first five minutes of class. Watch your students' reactions! Students can respond in the TL.

Student activity: Have students be quiet for five minutes. Have them write in the TL about their thoughts during the silence.

Creativity Starter 4 – Conga line

ACTFL: Culture: practices, Novice Mid; **CEFR:** A1

Teacher activity: Play the *Conga* song by Gloria Estefan from your smartphone or music list. Dance around the room as if leading a Conga line.

Students may comment in the TL while you dance.

Student activity: Have students do the Conga dance. Choose a student to lead the students around the room in song and dance. Students are to speak in the TL.

Creativity Starter 5 – Be a cheerleader

ACTFL: Presentational, Novice Mid; **CEFR:** A1

Teacher activity: Dress up as a cheerleader and lead a cheer in your world language. Keep wearing your outfit for the rest of the day.

Student activity: Have students repeat the cheer in the TL.

Choose several students to lead the cheer that you modeled above.

Creativity Starter 6 – Stand on the desk and recite poetry

ACTFL: Presentational, Intermediate Low; **CEFR:** A2

Teacher activity: Stand on top of your classroom desk and recite a famous poem by a great poet who is from a country where your world language is spoken. Students can respond in the TL. Be careful. Have two students help you get on and off the desk.

Student activity: Have students study a TL poem and recite the poem in pairs in the TL. Allow two students to recite the poem from atop your teacher desk!

Creativity Starter 7 – Classroom zoo

ACTFL: Interpersonal, Intermediate Low; **CEFR:** A2

Teacher activity: Dress as an animal such as a gorilla, panda, tiger, lion, wolf, parrot, eagle, etc. Allow students to ask you questions in your world language!

Student activity: Students are to role-play certain animals in a zoo. The rest of the students walk about the zoo and comment in the TL and speak to the animals in the TL. Allow students to dress up or use stuffed animals or puppets.

Creativity Starter 8 – Imaginary bus ride

ACTFL: Interpersonal (listening)/presentational (writing), Intermediate Mid; **CEFR:** B1

Teacher activity: You are the bus driver/tour guide. Have the class follow you around the room in a line while you drive the bus down some imaginary streets in a famous city in your world language country. Stop the bus whenever you want. Students are to speak in the TL while on the bus.

Student activity: Have students write an article in the TL for the school newspaper. The article describes the site you saw during your world language bus tour.

Creativity Starter 9 – Ghost time

ACTFL: Interpersonal/presentational, Intermediate Mid; **CEFR:** B1

Teacher activity: Dress like a ghost! Speak to the class only in your world language. Make-up a zany history about yourself and relate that to your students. Have them ask you questions in your world language.

Student activity: Allow students to role-play a ghost speaking to the school principal. One student is the ghost, the other is the principal. Students work in pairs. The ghost relates to the principal a problem they are having at school. Students speak in the TL.

Creativity Starter 10 – Celebrity dress-up day

ACTFL: Interpersonal/presentational, Intermediate High; **CEFR:** B1

Teacher activity: Dress up as a famous writer, painter, singer, actor, or athlete, etc. from your world language country. Speak only in your world language.

Have the students ask you questions in the TL.

Student activity: Have students prepare for a dress-up day. Have them be a famous writer, painter, singer, actor, or athlete, etc. They are to introduce themselves to the class and speak briefly about their life in the TL.

Creativity Starter 11 – Crazy commands

ACTFL: Presentational, Novice Mid; **CEFR:** A2

Teacher activity: Give students ten zany commands to do such as jump, hop on one leg, run in place, applaud, applaud with one hand, wave, leap, etc. Give the commands in your world language.

Student activity: Have students work in pairs and draw two commands for the class to act out. Have each pair lead the class in doing two zany commands in the TL.

Creativity Starter 12 – Exercise

ACTFL: Interpretive, Novice Mid; **CEFR:** A1

Teacher activity: Do some fun exercises for the class. Do a few toe touches, run in place, jumping jacks, etc. Count in your world language each time you do an exercise.

Do an online search to demonstrate with a real exercise class from an authentic site.

Student activity: Have students stand to do some fun exercises! Count each time they do an exercise, such as jumping jacks, running in place, arm stretches, etc. Use an online search to find an instructor doing some exercises in your world language.

Creativity Starter 13 – Animal sounds

ACTFL: Interpersonal/presentational, Novice Mid; **CEFR:** A1

Teacher activity: Imitate the sounds animals make in your world language. Students guess the animal in the TL.

Student activity: Have students bring in a stuffed animal to describe in the TL. Have them make the animal sound associated with their animal. Let the students do the work in pairs.

Creativity Starter 14 – Paper airplane

ACTFL: Presentational (writing) Interpretive (reading), Novice Mid; **CEFR:** A2

Teacher activity: Make five paper airplanes and include a written question on the airplane in your world language. Fly each airplane. The student who catches each plane gets to answer the question in his/her world language.

Student activity: Students make up a question in the TL and put the question onto a paper airplane they make. Students fly their planes to the person nearest them and that person answers the question in the TL and sends it back to the sender!

Creativity Starter 15 – Spring cleaning

ACTFL: Interpersonal/presentational, Intermediate Mid; **CEFR:** B1

Teacher activity: Dress up as a cleaning person/janitor and enter class. Have the class describe in pairs and in the TL, what you are cleaning. Bring rags, a vacuum, glass cleaner, etc.

Student activity: Allow students to work in pairs and make up a skit in the TL between a cleaning person/janitor and the owner of a house. Video the fun presentations.

Creativity Starter 16 – Zany incident

ACTFL: Interpretive/presentational, Intermediate Mid; **CEFR:** B1+

Teacher activity: Stage a funny incident using a couple of students in class.

This could be a comical robbery, a funny airplane ride, car accident, etc. Speak only in your world language.

Student activity: Students are to work in pairs and create a zany incident in the TL, then present the skits in front of the class.

Creativity Starter 17 – Karate lesson

ACTFL: Interpersonal/presentational, Novice Mid; **CEFR:** A1

Teacher activity: Dress up like a karate instructor. Wear an imaginary black belt. Teach the class a few moves in your world language! Have the class do the moves when possible. Everyone shouts out some fun words in the TL as they follow and repeat the words of their instructor in their world language.

Student activity: Have students work in pairs and invent a new karate move to teach to the class using the TL.

Creativity Starter 18 – What's in the suitcase?

ACTFL: Interpersonal, Novice High; **CEFR:** A2

Teacher activity: Bring in a suitcase that contains some strange items. Have students guess the items in the TL.

Student activity: Have a pair of students bring in one suitcase filled with surprises. The class guesses in the TL what the items are in the suitcase.

Creativity Starter 19 – Airplane pilot

ACTFL: Presentational, Novice High; **CEFR:** A2+

Teacher activity: Be an airplane pilot! Dress up and take the class around the room. Have students form one long line as they follow you around the room. Say in your world language the names of famous cities and countries as you speed across the world. Use commands and short fun expressions in your world language!

Student activity: Have the students sit down and draw pictures of some of the places you visited. Have them write some commands beneath the drawings in the world language.

Creativity Starter 20 – Art museum

ACTFL: Intepretive (listening), Novice High; **CEFR:** A2+

Teacher activity: Be a museum guide. Project a photo of a famous art museum in a city where your world language is spoken. Show three more pictures of famous paintings in the museum. Speak in your world language. Have the class stand and move about as if they are in an actual museum.

Student activity: Have students sit down and draw their own interpretation of one of the three paintings on the screen.

Decorate the classroom with the drawings and give your class a famous museum name. Drawings should be zany and creative!

Creativity Starter 21 – Beach day

ACTFL: Interpersonal, Novice High; **CEFR:** A2

Teacher activity: Dress up wearing beach apparel that includes a funny hat and sunglasses. Have students describe in the TL where you are, what you are wearing, and what you are doing.

Student activity: Invite students to join you on the imaginary beach and practice the TL while speaking in pairs. Have some food. Play some music.

Creativity Starter 22 – Dance time

ACTFL: Culture: practices, all levels; **CEFR:** —

Teacher activity: Be a famous dancer from one of your TL countries. Dress the role. Put on music to a famous song in your world language and show your students some of your moves! Have them applaud and dance in place while standing next to their desks.

Student activity: Ask students to stand, applaud, and dance with you as if they were watching you in concert. Ask students to volunteer and dance along with you.

Creativity Starter 23 – Great singer

ACTFL: Presentational, Novice Mid; **CEFR:** A1

Teacher activity: Be a famous singer from one of your TL countries. Lip sync a famous song by the celebrity TL singer. Have the class stand and sing along in the TL. Have them applaud, etc.

Student activity: Ask students to work in pairs. Let them pick their favorite singer and song from a world language country. Have them lip sync in pairs!

They may use tablets, laptops, etc. to listen to and watch the singer selected.

Creativity Starter 24 – Be a superhero

ACTFL: Interpersonal/presentational, Novice Mid; **CEFR:** A1

Teacher activity: Dress up as a superhero. Try Superman, Batman, Spider-Man, Wonder Woman, Superwoman, etc. Have students stand and have them follow around the room as if you were flying, in your Batmobile or sending out webs, etc. It is OK to wave arms as if flying.

Practice some fun expressions in your world language while flying.

Student activity: Have students make their own superhero puppets. They can use socks or paper bags. Have students work in pairs.

They are to say the name of their puppets in the TL and say what their special power is.

My Creativity Starter

Teacher activity:

Student activity:

12

Positivity, Celebration, and Final Thoughts

Introduction

This chapter is dedicated to **positivity and celebration.** It asks, "What have you done with the activities in this book?" It also contains ideas to help create and then plan a **positivity/celebration event** to celebrate your creative successes. CELEBRATIONS are a NECESSARY part of creativity. Successes should be celebrated, and celebrations encourage continued creativity. Give yourself a pat on the back for a job well done, and reward others who helped you get there! Remember, positivity and celebration translate into super-promotion for your world language program, administrators, world language teachers, students, community, and parents!

There are 23 suggested awards to give, as well as printable certificate templates to use. At the end are some final thoughts (reflections and advice) from the authors.

Let's Get Started

Let's be POSITIVE and let's CELEBRATE!

Each creative idea is a treasure, not to be lost in our creative journey.

Let's remember our successes and make our creative journey **the reason we are here and why we teach!**

Be the one who can say, **"I DID IT! I WAS CREATIVE!!!"**

Let's start **ending our sentences with exclamation points instead of periods!** It is fine to include three exclamation points once in a while.

While we are at it, let's sometimes end sentences with **ten exclamation points!!!!!!!!!!**

Let's also try to do **at least one Positivity Celebration** for those who help us. For some added celebration, see the Special Note below.

Let's make others and ourselves feel really good! Let's recognize and celebrate creativity!

HAVE FUN!

Special Note: Teachers may present the awards in each category only to their students and supporters, or the entire world language department could have a special awards night toward the end of the school year. **You can call the night World Language Awards Night** and invite everyone. Or make it **World Languages Oscar Night**! Have world language students perform in all languages in skits, poetry readings, songs, native dress, play musical instruments, etc. Place each award/certificate into a nice frame before presenting the awards. Have everyone dress up and walk on the red carpet. Take videos of the highlights of the events. Send the videoclips to local TV stations. Post pictures and videos on social media. Send pictures and descriptors of the special event to local newspapers. Include all digitally for the online newspapers. Be sure to invite the Principal, Assistant Principal, deans, counselors, coaches, band directors. Go for it! Invite the mayor of the city, the governor, the city council, or TV celebrities! Write an article for a world language publication about your special night. Have everyone dress up. Wear tuxes and gowns if you really want to be fancy!

Credit for illustration art on each award certificate © Skypix | Dreamstime.com

Positivity – Celebration 1

Teacher Colleague Support of the Year Award
Who are the colleagues who have inspired you to be creative? Take a moment to recognize them with a special acknowledgment. Invite them to lunch, a cup of coffee, an afternoon tea. Let them know you appreciate them! Tell them how they have helped you. Offer your creative teacher support to a fellow teacher! Honor them with a "World Language Teacher Colleague Support Award at the end of the school year!

Positivity – Celebration 2

World Language Student Support of the Year Award
Invite some of your students to an after school thank you celebration. Invite students who have helped you with technology, decorating the room and bulletin boards, housekeeping details, tutoring other students, giving you some creative ideas to use in the world language classroom.

Have a world language dish to honor these student supporters.

Honor them with a World Language Student Support Award at the end of the school year!

Positivity – Celebration 3

World Language Parental Support of the Year Award
Have a special after-school culture event for your parent supporters. Invite those parents who have helped you with housekeeping chores in your classroom, tutored students, presented sessions on world language topics, and promote world language study in your school. Have some food and refreshments.

Honor them with a World Language Parental Support Award during and/or at the end of the school year!

Positivity – Celebration 4

World Language Administrative Support of the Year Award
Invite some administrators who have supported you throughout the year to an afternoon or evening world language event to honor a counselor, an Assistant Principal, Principal, Dean of Students, Superintendent, or a School Board member. Honor the administrative supporters with a **World Language Administrative Support Award!**

Invite your students and parents to be guests. Provide drinks and chips. Let students perform some skits in their world language and sing some songs in their world languages. You may choose to make these awards at the end of the school year at the **World Language Awards Night!**

Positivity – Celebration 5

World Language Community Support of the Year Award
Invite some members of the community, such as business leaders who have supported you by being guest speakers, scholarship supporters for student trips, or scholarship supporters for college students who plan to study world languages. These supporters may include politicians in the community such as mayor, governor, senator, local, state, and national representatives as well as local TV celebrities such as athletes, TV anchors, local authors, musicians, or actors!

Honor the community supporters with a **World Language Community Support Award** at the end of the year **World Language Awards Night!**

Positivity – Celebration 6

World Language Creative Modes of Instruction of the Year Award
Have an end-of-school world language department ceremony after school or in the evening. Use the school and invite some parents, administrators, and students. Have appetizers and refreshments. Honor the world language teacher who had the best creative mode of instruction plan with the **World Language Creative Mode of Instruction Award for the School Year** at the **World Language Awards Night**. Refer to Mode of Instruction Category 1 found in Chapter Five of this book for modes of instruction used throughout the school year.

Positivity – Celebration 7

World Language Creative Teaching Ideas of the Year Award
Present this award at the end of the school year **World Language Awards Night!**

Award various teachers in your world language department for their use of the Category 2 Teaching Ideas section in Chapter 5 of this book. Review various ideas used by the teachers throughout the school year.

Present the **Most Creative Teaching Ideas Award of the Year** to deserving teachers!

Positivity – Celebration 8

World Language Promotional Ideas of the Year Award
Invite all supporters of the world language department to the end-of-the-year **World Language Awards Night!** These supporters may include politicians in the community such as mayor, governor, senator, local, state, and national representatives as well as local TV celebrities such as athletes, TV anchors, local authors, musicians, and actors. Honor those who promoted world language study in your school with a **World Language Promotion Award**.

Consider offering this award to various groups of world language supporters. There could also be promoters of world language from parents, students, and world language teachers. Many may qualify for this honor.

Consider giving the award to one or two people in each category. Let's make people feel **appreciated for their promotion!**

Refer to Chapter 5, Category 3 for reviewing possible promotional ideas used by various people.

Positivity – Celebration 9

World Language Teacher Creativity Starter of the Year Award
Present the **World Language Creativity Starter Award** at the end of the school year at **World Language Awards Night**. This award should go to the teacher(s) who has/have had the most creative starters for their classes throughout the school year. Please refer to Chapter 9 of this book for ideas on what starters have been used.

Positivity – Celebration 10

World Language Teacher Creativity Improvement of the Year Award
This may be the most important award for the teacher. Select one teacher in each world language taught at your school. Present each of them a **World Language Teacher Creativity Award** for their creative abilities. Please take into consideration those teachers who have IMPROVED their creativity during the year. If necessary, award an extra award to a second teacher in each language. Present these awards at the **World Language Awards Night** at the end of the school year.

Positivity – Celebration 11

World Language Student Academic Achievement of the Year Award
Present one of these awards to a student in each of the world languages taught in your school. You may want to offer this award for each level of language offered: Level 1, Level 2, Level 3, Level 4, and Level 5. Give these awards at the **World Language Awards Night** at the end of the school year. These awards should be given for academic achievement in each world language. This achievement includes the students' final grade (percent) each semester in the world language being studied.

Positivity – Celebration 12

World Language Positive Attitude of the Year Award
Award one or two students in each world language this award. This award recognizes those students who were always positive in class. Their attitudes were a reflection of enthusiasm and positivity. The words *complain* and *bored* were never in their vocabulary. They inspired all with their positivity and enthusiasm. Present these awards on **World Language Awards Night** at the end of the school year!

Positivity – Celebration 13

World Language Creative Student of the Year Award
Present one of these awards to a student in each of the world languages taught in your school. These students are the highly creative students in your classes. These students invent new ideas, try out new ideas while

doing world language projects or while acting out world language skits. These students are not afraid to risk-take. They love being CREATIVE! They motivate others as they often share their creativity with fellow students and teachers.

Present these awards at the **World Language Awards Night** at the end of the school year.

Positivity – Celebration 14

World Language Student Behavior of the Year Award
Award one or two students in each world language this award. This award recognizes those students who always behaved properly. They always arrived to class on time and followed classroom rules. You never had to correct their behavior. They followed directions throughout the year.

They made your job tolerable and fun! They inspired others by their high level of exemplary behavior! Present these awards on **World Language Awards Night** at the end of the school year!!!

Positivity – Celebration 15

World Language Speaker of the Year Award
Award one or two students in each world language this award for best speaker of their world language. These students excelled at speaking the world language. They also motivated others to speak in the world language! They spoke in their world language during class skits, literary readings, question/answer sessions, during class discussion of topics, etc.

Present these awards at the end-of-the-year **World Language Awards Night!!!**

Positivity – Celebration 16

World Language Reader of the Year Award
Give this award to the top reader in each world language. These students are your top readers. They love reading in their world language. They read and think in their world language. These students are super-positive about reading. They choose to read books in the TL in their free time. They always volunteer to read in their world language. Present these awards at the end-of-the-year **World Language Awards Night!!!**

Positivity – Celebration 17

World Language Writer of the Year Award
Present this writing award to a student in each world language who, through the course of the year, has written superior short stories, essays, poems or plays in their world language. Mention what they did and ask the students to read a short excerpt from what they wrote. Award these honors at **World Language Awards Night**!

Positivity – Celebration 18

World Language Grammar Student of the Year Award
Present a student from each world language the "World Language Grammar Student of the Year" award. These students are experts at world language grammar. They rarely make a mistake when using grammar in their world language while speaking or writing. They are indeed the top grammarians in their world language. They always get an A on their grammar tests. Present these awards at **World Language Awards Night**!

Positivity – Celebration 19

World Language Student Techie of the Year Award
Give a student from each world language the "World Language Student Techie of the Year" award. This can include the invention of a fun game, a new world language app, a super world language website set up by students, a world language blog, a special project and many more. Ask students to present a brief summary of their projects at **World Language Awards Night**!

Positivity – Celebration 20

World Language Social Media Student of the Year Award
Present a student from each world language the "World Language Social Media Student of the Year" award. This can include the use of Facebook,

Instagram, TikTok, and YouTube to promote world language. These uses of social media could be to promote world language via video clips from smartphones that highlight special world language projects, trips, awards ceremonies, etc. Ask students to present a brief summary of their use of social media at **World Language Awards Night**!

Positivity – Celebration 21

World Language Most Improved Academic Achievement of the Year Award
Award the "Most Improvement in World Language Study" award to a student in each world language who, through the course of the year, has demonstrated superior improvement in the world language classroom for her/his/their academic achievements! Honor the efforts, dedication, and perseverance of these special students. Award these honors at **World Language Awards Night**!

Positivity – Celebration 22

World Language Most Improved Student Behavior of the Year Award
Give this award to a student in each world language who, through the course of the year, has demonstrated superior improvement in their behavior in the world language classroom. Honor the efforts, dedication, and perseverance of these special students to improve their conduct. Mention what they did and how they improved over the course of the year. Award these honors at **World Language Awards Night**!

Positivity – Celebration 23

World Language Culture Project of the Year Award
Award the **"Outstanding World Language Project of the Year"** to a student or group of students who completed a truly outstanding culture project. You may wish to include students from each TL. Refer to Chapter 8 for culture project ideas you may want to include if the students utilized some of those during the course of the year. Ask students to present a brief summary of their projects at **World Language Awards Night**! This could include a song, a dance, a special recipe, and more.

Teacher Colleague Support of the Year Award

Name of Teacher Colleague _____

In recognition of your creative and consistent teacher support of world language teachers in their march toward creativity! THANKS!!!

Signature - World Language Teacher _____

Signature - World Language Director _____

Signature - School Principal _____

Copyright material from Deborah Blaz and Tom Alsop (2023), *Sparking Creativity in the World Language Classroom: Strategies and Ideas to Build Your Students' Language Skills*, Routledge.

World Language Student Support of the Year Award

Name of Student _____

In recognition of your creative and consistent student support of a world language teacher in their march toward creativity! THANKS!!!

Date awarded _____

Signature - World Language Teacher _____

Signature - World Language Director _____

Signature - School Principal _____

Copyright material from Deborah Blaz and Tom Alsop (2023), *Sparking Creativity in the World Language Classroom: Strategies and Ideas to Build Your Students' Language Skills*, Routledge.

World Language Parental Support of the Year Award

Name of Parent _____

In recognition of your creative and consistent parental support of a world language teacher in their march toward creativity! THANKS!!!

Date awarded _____

Signature - World Language Teacher _____

Signature - World Language Director _____

Signature - School Principal _____

Copyright material from Deborah Blaz and Tom Alsop (2023), *Sparking Creativity in the World Language Classroom: Strategies and Ideas to Build Your Students' Language Skills,* Routledge.

World Language Administrative Support of the Year Award

Name of Administrator _____

In recognition of your creative and consistent administrative support of world language teachers in their march toward creativity! THANKS!!!

Date awarded _____

Signature - World Language Teacher _____

Signature - World Language Director _____

Signature - School Principal _____

Copyright material from Deborah Blaz and Tom Alsop (2023), *Sparking Creativity in the World Language Classroom: Strategies and Ideas to Build Your Students' Language Skills,* Routledge.

World Language Community Support of the Year Award

Name of Supporter _____

In recognition of your creative and consistent community support of world language teachers in their march toward creativity! THANKS!!!

Date awarded _____

Signature – World Language Teacher _____

Signature – World Language Director _____

Signature – School Principal _____

World Language Creative Modes of Instruction of the Year Award

Name of Teacher _____

In recognition of your consistent use of creative modes of instruction in the world language classroom! Those modes of instruction have helped you and others in your march to creativity! THANKS!!!

Date awarded _____

Signature - World Language Teacher _____

Signature - World Language Director _____

Signature - School Principal _____

Copyright material from Deborah Blaz and Tom Alsop (2023), *Sparking Creativity in the World Language Classroom: Strategies and Ideas to Build Your Students' Language Skills,* Routledge.

World Language Creative Teaching Ideas of the Year Award

Name of Teacher _____

In recognition of your consistent use of creative teaching ideas in the world language classroom! Those teaching ideas have helped you and others in your march to creativity! THANKS!!!

Date awarded _____

Signature – World Language Teacher _____

Signature – World Language Director _____

Signature – School Principal _____

Copyright material from Deborah Blaz and Tom Alsop (2023), *Sparking Creativity in the World Language Classroom: Strategies and Ideas to Build Your Students' Language Skills*, Routledge.

World Language Promotional Ideas of the Year Award

Name _____

In recognition of your consistent offering of promotional ideas to foster the continued study of world languages! Those promotional ideas have helped you and others toward your march to creativity! THANKS!!!

Date awarded _____

Signature - World Language Teacher _____

Signature - World Language Director _____

Signature - School Principal _____

Copyright material from Deborah Blaz and Tom Alsop (2023), *Sparking Creativity in the World Language Classroom: Strategies and Ideas to Build Your Students' Language Skills*, Routledge.

World Language Teacher Creativity Starter of the Year Award

Name of Teacher _____

In recognition of your consistent use of successful starters in your march toward creativity! That creativity has helped you and others toward your march to creativity! THANKS!!!

Date awarded _____

Signature - World Language Teacher _____

Signature - World Language Director _____

Signature - School Principal _____

Copyright material from Deborah Blaz and Tom Alsop (2023), *Sparking Creativity in the World Language Classroom: Strategies and Ideas to Build Your Students' Language Skills*, Routledge.

World Language Teacher Creativity Improvement of the Year Award

Name of Teacher _____

In recognition of your consistent use of creativity in your world language classroom! That creativity has helped you and others in your march toward creativity! THANKS!!!

Date awarded _____

Signature - World Language Teacher _____

Signature - World Language Director _____

Signature - School Principal _____

Copyright material from Deborah Blaz and Tom Alsop (2023), *Sparking Creativity in the World Language Classroom: Strategies and Ideas to Build Your Students' Language Skills,* Routledge.

World Language Student Academic Achievement of the Year Award

Name of Student _____

In recognition of your outstanding grades in your world language class. Those study habits have helped you and others in your march toward creativity! THANKS!!!

Date awarded _____

Signature - World Language Teacher _____

Signature - World Language Director _____

Signature - School Principal _____

Copyright material from Deborah Blaz and Tom Alsop (2023), *Sparking Creativity in the World Language Classroom: Strategies and Ideas to Build Your Students' Language Skills,* Routledge.

World Language Positive Attitude of the Year Award

Name of Student _____

In recognition of your consistent positive attitude in your world language class. That positivity has helped you and others in your march toward creativity! THANKS!!!

Date awarded _____

Signature - World Language Teacher _____

Signature - World Language Director _____

Signature - School Principal _____

Copyright material from Deborah Blaz and Tom Alsop (2023), *Sparking Creativity in the World Language Classroom: Strategies and Ideas to Build Your Students' Language Skills,* Routledge.

World Language Creative Student of the Year Award

Name of Student _____

In recognition of your creativity in your world language class. That creativity has helped you and others in your march toward creativity! THANKS!!!

Date awarded _____

Signature - World Language Teacher _____

Signature - World Language Director _____

Signature - School Principal _____

World Language Student Behavior of the Year Award

Name of Student _____

In recognition of outstanding behavior in your world language class. That behavior has helped you in your march toward creativity! THANKS!!!

Date awarded _____

Signature - World Language Teacher _____

Signature - World Language Director _____

Signature - School Principal _____

Copyright material from Deborah Blaz and Tom Alsop (2023), *Sparking Creativity in the World Language Classroom: Strategies and Ideas to Build Your Students' Language Skills,* Routledge.

World Language Speaker of the Year Award

Name of Student _____

In recognition of your outstanding ability to speak in your world language. This ability has helped you and others in your march toward creativity! THANKS!!!

Date awarded _____

Signature - World Language Teacher _____

Signature - World Language Director _____

Signature - School Principal _____

Copyright material from Deborah Blaz and Tom Alsop (2023), *Sparking Creativity in the World Language Classroom: Strategies and Ideas to Build Your Students' Language Skills,* Routledge.

World Language Reader of the Year Award

Name of Student _____

In recognition of your outstanding ability to read in your world language. This ability has helped you in your march toward creativity! THANKS!!!

Date awarded _____

Signature - World Language Teacher _____

Signature - World Language Director _____

Signature - School Principal _____

Copyright material from Deborah Blaz and Tom Alsop (2023), *Sparking Creativity in the World Language Classroom: Strategies and Ideas to Build Your Students' Language Skills,* Routledge.

World Language Writer of the Year Award

Name of Student _____

In recognition of your outstanding writing! That writing has helped you and others better understand written creativity in the world language! THANKS!!!

Date awarded _____

Signature - World Language Teacher _____

Signature - World Language Director _____

Signature - School Principal _____

World Language Grammar Student of the Year Award

Name of Student _____

In recognition of your outstanding abilities in grammar usage in your world language. Your knowledge of grammar will help you be successful in your march toward creativity! THANKS!!!

Date awarded _____

Signature - World Language Teacher _____

Signature - World Language Director _____

Signature - School Principal _____

World Language Student Techie of the Year Award

Name of Student _____

In recognition of your outstanding abilities to use technology in the world language classroom. That techie talent has helped you and others in your march toward creativity! THANKS!!!

Date awarded _____

Signature - World Language Teacher _____

Signature - World Language Director _____

Signature - School Principal _____

Copyright material from Deborah Blaz and Tom Alsop (2023), *Sparking Creativity in the World Language Classroom: Strategies and Ideas to Build Your Students' Language Skills*, Routledge.

Positivity, Celebration, and Final Thoughts ◆ 265

World Language Social Media Student of the Year Award

Name of Student _____

In recognition of your outstanding abilities using social media in your world language class. That use has helped you and others in your march toward creativity! THANKS!!!

Date awarded _____

Signature - World Language Teacher _____

Signature - World Language Director _____

Signature - School Principal _____

Copyright material from Deborah Blaz and Tom Alsop (2023), *Sparking Creativity in the World Language Classroom: Strategies and Ideas to Build Your Students' Language Skills,* Routledge.

World Language Most Improved Academic Achievement of the Year Award

Name of Student _____

In recognition of your improvement in academic achievement in world language class. That dedication to your study of world language has helped you in your march toward creativity! THANKS!!!

Date awarded _____

Signature - World Language Teacher _____

Signature - World Language Director _____

Signature - School Principal _____

Positivity, Celebration, and Final Thoughts ◆ 267

World Language Most Improved Student Behavior of the Year Award

Name of Student _____

In recognition of your improvement in behavior while in your world language class. Continue to improve your behavior in your march toward creativity! THANKS!!!

Date awarded _____

Signature - World Language Teacher _____

Signature - World Language Director _____

Signature - School Principal _____

Copyright material from Deborah Blaz and Tom Alsop (2023), *Sparking Creativity in the World Language Classroom: Strategies and Ideas to Build Your Students' Language Skills*, Routledge.

World Language Culture Project of the Year Award

Name of Student _____

In recognition of your outstanding culture project completed in your world language class. Your love for culture has helped you in your march toward creativity! THANKS!!!

Date awarded _____

Signature - World Language Teacher _____

Signature - World Language Director _____

Signature - School Principal _____

Copyright material from Deborah Blaz and Tom Alsop (2023), *Sparking Creativity in the World Language Classroom: Strategies and Ideas to Build Your Students' Language Skills,* Routledge.

Final Thoughts

Remember that being creative is not a destination – it is all about the *process*:

- Why is it important to you to be creative? Set a goal for yourself: what do you need? Or, what do the students need? The best way to approach this is by anticipating the joy you will feel in creating something new. (Chapter 1)
- Use your imagination (your "sparks") about what might achieve that goal. (Chapters 3 and 4)
- Then, get creative. What actions need to happen? (Chapters 5, 6, 7, 10 and 11)
- Establish a support system. (Chapter 8)
- Try out your idea and HAVE FUN while doing so! Enthusiasm and joy are contagious!
- Persist; it is okay if your first try isn't perfect. You aren't doing this to be famous or become rich. You are doing it because it is fun! (Chapter 9)
- Reflect and evaluate: what went well, and what could be improved? How will you know if you achieved your goal? (Chapter 9)
- Whatever the results, celebrate the process as described in this chapter. Small daily rewards might be best.

You can fill your head with excuses: no time to try anything new, too many demands on us, fear of what others may think, etc. Throw out such ideas. You know in your heart you can do this, but break things down into small, manageable chunks, if possible.

Don't be rigid (as if to give yourself "homework," such as "I must do this every week") – do it only if it's enjoyable (if you're not excited, it's hard to get your students excited about trying something). I like Albert Einstein's statement: "Creativity is intelligence having fun."

Set the bar low and keep it low. Again, this is supposed to be rewarding and fun. Too much of anything gets old fast, or becomes more of a chore. Take baby steps (once each semester, once each level, etc.) – whatever approach doesn't sound too scary for you.

Go through the process ALL THE WAY. You will learn and grow so much.

No matter what happens, your life will be enriched by trying to be creative. Go forth and sparkle.

Appendix
Standards Correlations

ACTFL, CEFR, CCSS, DOK

For those using the Common Core (CCSS) or Depth of Knowledge (DOK), here is a chart summarizing and comparing the ACTFL proficiency levels to those of the CEFR and CCSS, according to the ACTFL:

ACTFL	CEFR	CCSS	DOK*
Novice Low	—	—	1
Novice Mid	—	R 2, SL 1	1
Novice High	A1	R 2, W 6, SL 1	1
Intermediate Low	A2	R 1, W 6, SL 1	2
Intermediate Mid	A2+	R 5; W 6, 8; SL 1, 4, 5, 6	2, 3
Intermediate High	B1	R 4; W 3, 4, 5, 6, 8; SL 4, 5, 6	3
Advanced Low	B1+	R 6; W 6, 8; SL 2, 4, 6	3, 4
Advanced Mid	B2	R 3, 7; W 2, 6, 7; SL 4, 6	4
Advanced High	C1	R 8, 9; W 6, 7, 10; SL 5	4
Superior	C2	R 10, W 9, SL 3	4
Distinguished	C2	R, W, SL all	4

*Depth of Knowledge standards are:
- Level 1 (Acquired Knowledge) involves recall and reproduction tasks such as remembering words or grammar rules.
- Level 2 (Knowledge Application) focuses on skills rather than discreet knowledge as well as concepts such as gender, tenses, cultural topics, etc. Students must choose the appropriate method to use a verb or construct a sentence, making decisions and completing teachable steps (sentence position, etc.).
- Level 3 (Analysis) involves strategic thinking, which means developing a plan on how to do something that has more than one possible response or solution.
- Level 4 (Augmentation) is extended thinking, or analyzing, evaluating, and possibly synthesizing several sources to give an opinion or generate an idea.

As such, it is possible to do activities for levels 2, 3, and perhaps 4 even at the Novice level, but since the majority of the Novice level expectations fit the definition of Level 1, the DOK in this chart is listed according to what the majority of proficiencies are for that level.

Sources

Achor, S. (2011). *The happiness advantage: the seven principles that fuel success and performance at work.* London: Virgin.

American Council for the Teaching of Foreign Languages. (2012). *Aligning CCSS languages standards – ACTFL.* Alignment of the National Standards for Learning Languages. Retrieved July 18, 2022, from https://www.actfl.org/sites/default/files/news/AligningCCSSLanguageStandards.pdf

Burgess, D. (2018). *Teach like a pirate: Increase student engagement, boost your creativity, and transform your life as an educator.* San Diego, CA: Dave Burgess Consulting, Inc.

Pringle, Z.I. (2020). Creativity requires taking risks. *Psychology Today.* Retrieved June 23, 2022, from https://www.psychologytoday.com/us/blog/creativity-the-art-and-science/202011/creativity-requires-taking-risks

Rodriguez, T. (2012). Creativity predicts a longer life. *Scientific American.* Retrieved June 24, 2022, from https://www.scientificamerican.com/article/open-mind-longer-life/

Image Source Credits

Icon 1 (Chapter 2): Map – Royalty Free Image
Icon 2 (Chapters 5, 6, 7): Space Capsule – TOPVECTORSTOCK – Dreamstime.com
Icon 3 (Chapter 8): Support Tree – Royalty Free Image
Icon 4 (Chapter 8): Computer – Daboost – Dreamstime.com
Icon 5 (Chapters 1, 2, 3, 4, 5, 6, 7, 8, 9, 10, 11, 12): Sparkler – Royalty Free Image
Icon 10A (Chapter 10): Cook – Cory Thoman – Dreamstime.com
Icon 10B (Chapter 10): Cook – Christos Georghiou – Dreamstime.com
Icon 10C (Chapter 10): Cook – Libux77 – Dreamstime.com
Icon 12.1 (Chapter 12): Thank You – Skypix – Dreamstime.com
Icon 12.2 (Cover and Chapter 12): Hands with Sparklers – Phive 2015 – Dreamstime.com

For Product Safety Concerns and Information please contact our EU representative GPSR@taylorandfrancis.com
Taylor & Francis Verlag GmbH, Kaufingerstraße 24, 80331 München, Germany

www.ingramcontent.com/pod-product-compliance
Lightning Source LLC
Chambersburg PA
CBHW080935300426

44115CB00017B/2826